SELF-HELP MANUAL

TO BE
PERFECT
IS
EASY

ARTHUR HILL & OSWALD HOWARD

TO BE PERFECT IS

EASY

SELF-HELP MANUAL

Arthur Hill & Oswald Howard

INTRODUCTION

Arthur Hill and Oswald Howard are two practicing psychologists with extensive experience in personality psychology. The problems of personal self-development are the cornerstone in psychology. This work opens the veil of the basic concepts that are so important in improving the personality on the path to self-development.

"To be perfect is easy" can be useful not only for practicing psychologists, but also for people who seek to be more confident and successful in their lives or who are trying to cope with difficult situations, depressions, to overcome self-doubt or to fill their lives with positive emotions.

Boredom and fear, difficulty in making decisions, a state of constant stress, self-deception, an illusory view of life, uncontrollable emotions - each of us faces this in everyday life.

In self-help manual, we explain the causes and consequences of the aforementioned negative psychological states of a person and possible ways to cope with them.

We are confident that the recitation of this book will be able to structure your life and to overcome internal divisions, to get rid of unnecessary doubts, to develop your intuition and to achieve success in self-development.

PREFACE

Stages of personality development is one of the most interesting and popular topics. This is due to the desire of the individual to learn something secret about himself and to become someone even more advanced.

The main criterion for comparing the stages of personality development is the refinement of perception. The finer the perception, the more subtle shades and faces the person is able to behold in any phenomenon. The second criterion for comparing the stages of personality development is foresight, or otherwise - wisdom. The wiser a person is, the more he filters the content of his own mind, and the less he gives in to gross impulses. The third and perhaps the most interesting criterion for comparing the stages of personality development is admission to spheres. This is manifested as the permission of the "participants" of the sphere to stay in their society, which lives according to certain official or unwritten laws.

A new level of awareness kills the current level of "I" so that the "I" is reborn more refined, strong and adapted to this level of awareness. This is a painful, but very fast way to self-development.

Almost no one understands that mentally adults are not among us. Therefore, everyone is shaking over his personal insecurity, as if over secret leprosy, which, by all means, must be hidden from everyone. Almost everyone implicitly believes that he is such a helpless coward - alone, and the rest live in an adult world that you need to be able to reach out to show that you are worthy of him.

But we are not ready to admit our insecurity and helplessness, because we continue to blindly believe in the fictitious world of worthy, self-confident, adult people, who are supposed to somehow fit in. And then everything will be "OK."

Desire - is the energy of the individual. Desires charge, give strength to move. If you are not an enlightened Buddha, a desireless, purposeless life will seem like a tragic path to nowhere. No strength to step into such a future remains.

It may seem that desire is a fragile shield from the all-embracing depressing meaninglessness of life. They say that you need to find and catch meanings, and depression is a natural state: always behind you, stalks, and you should stumble, lose relationships, meaningful acquaintances, work - and it will absorb.And this is an illusion.

No matter how difficult the situation may be, if I am sure that tomorrow, in a month, or even a year, happiness will return, then there will be no depression. Sometimes you just don't notice what you believe in, how you look forward to tomorrow.

There are many sagging neuroses in the psyche, they absorb the territory of consciousness. At the same time, the channel of perception narrows, and any intense emotions completely obscure it, loading all thoughts with its energy. As a result, everything that a person is worried about becomes for him the ultimate objective reality - even the most outspoken chimeras are taken at face value. What kind of cinema the mind shows, such a life is perceived without any doubt.

Contents

Psychology of personality development

Stages of personality development is one of the most interesting and popular topics. This is due to the desire of the individual to learn something secret about himself and to become someone even more advanced. Reading about the stages of development, we mentally determine our place in life, and look at the nearby perspective. This may be an intermediate stage between clearly defined stages, or some specific stage. As a rule, in systems describing the stages of development, there are three initial stages along which social people move, one transitional stage, and two or three levels of the spiritual level. In this article I will not make large deviations from the usual canons, but I will try to present my view on the **stages of the development of personality and consciousness**.

First of all, I would like to say that there is nothing wrong with being at one or another stage. Everyone from birth is forced to go through the stages of personality development. And if you jump over a step somewhere, most likely the experience will be incomplete, and you will have to catch up. It is foolish to blame a first-grader for not being able to solve the problems of the university. If, in your opinion, a person is stupid, perhaps in his life there have not been those lessons thanks to which he could gain wisdom. And in your life there were no lessons that eliminate the roots of the energy-consuming habit - to condemn. In a developed person, soul, stage by stage, has come a long way. The current stage of development depends on past experience.

All people are different - each at its own stage, and the concept of rebirths of the soul could best explain this phenomenon. It seems like - the past is unknown, and therefore the result of the past in the form of the current stage of development must be taken for granted. The acceptability of such an explanation depends on the personal worldview. If we omit the theory of reincarnation, then we can say that the developed personality was lucky - probably she had good genes and living conditions suitable for development.

It makes no sense to condemn people who are "undeveloped" regarding our level. If a person at his stage of development is weak and cannot solve a problem that seems elementary to us, this means that we are "more lucky" - we have received better upbringing and education. If a person avoids difficulties, then he is either not ready for them, or "not lucky", and he still does not comprehend what lesson can give an independent solution to problems.

There are no objectively high and low stages of development - everything is relative. And if you become attached to these ranks, there will always be a man on earth who will be two heads taller than your person, in comparison with which our stage will turn out to be low. The fewer games of exaltation and humiliation, the less empty energy waste on a sense of self-importance. However, in our scale of six stages of the development of personality and consciousness, I will proceed from the middle levels, to which a large part of the world's population is involved, and call the subsequent stages (relatively characteristic of most people) high levels of personality development.

A person who is at a certain stage of development may have missed lessons from previous stages, which at times can pop up in the form of a temporary regression. There may also be developments from the advanced stages of development - local heights that contribute to an evolutionary career like beacons on the way.

Criteria for development

The main criterion for comparing the stages of personality development is the refinement of perception. The finer the perception, the more subtle shades and faces the person is able to behold in any phenomenon. The grosser the perception, the less legible the person. What is normal for a person at the first stage of development will seem rude (depending on the situation: stupid, inappropriate, ineffective, too straightforward) for a more advanced person. And in fact, all of the following is a slightly more detailed description of how the process of perception is refined from the transition from one stage of personality development to another. On this topic on progressman.ru there are a number of articles under the tag "sensitivity".

The second criterion for comparing the stages of personality development is foresight, or otherwise - wisdom. The wiser a person is, the more he filters the content of his own mind, and the less he gives in to gross impulses. Such a person knows that if you tolerate a little in the present and work on yourself, the future will not make you disappointed in yourself. Conversely, a short-sighted person is unreasonably wasting energy and resources in order to satisfy himself quickly, without worrying about the future.

The third and perhaps the most interesting criterion for comparing the stages of personality development is admission to spheres. This is manifested as the permission of the "participants" of the sphere to stay in their society, which lives according to certain official or unwritten laws. The finer the perception and the higher the stage of development, the more subtle and reasonable laws a person accepts, and the stricter the adherence to these laws. If, for example, a person wants to have close contact with peaceful and honest people, he himself must become honest and peaceful, then this area will accept him.

The first stage of personality development

This is the stage of a rude person, whose main interests are almost no different from the interests of animals. Of course, survival, sex and gluttony in the human body are clothed in complex social guises, and are surrounded by rituals, but the essence remains unchanged. There is a basic need that eclipses consciousness, and there is a way to this need. If a person at the first stage of development is not overgrown with social qualities, the path to fulfilling these needs is simplified. The less social the personality at the first stage of development, the closer the person's behavior is to the animal.

Social barriers in a person's mind, as a rule, block primitive instincts and place a kind of mental buffer between consciousness and need. The less a person of the first stages of development is civilized, the stronger the power of his instincts is manifested, and the more rude and straightforward will be the fulfillment of his needs. In society, this translates into violence and immoral behavior.

Sometimes a gross desire at the first stage of personality development overshadows consciousness, and a person doesn't care - just to satisfy this desire. He does not pay attention to the idea that there can be retribution for rude behavior. The strength of desire and the anticipation of its fulfillment can overpower the subtle awareness of thoughts about the consequences. This is the absence of awareness, wisdom and foresight.

At the first stage of personality development, a person almost does not realize that killing and violence are behavior that must be avoided if a person does not want to become like animals and live according to their laws. The only thing that holds him back is the fear of punishment and, to a lesser extent, moral values. This happens due to the fact that perception itself at this level is coarse, dull, and therefore a person does not comprehend the third criterion for the development of personality associated with admission to areas that live according to certain laws.

Moreover, a person at this level, to some extent, can distinguish other stages of personality development as more subtle and desirable. But he completely lacks the realization that the transition to a new level is associated with understanding and observing the laws of more subtle stages of development. Nobody wants violence against themselves, and in order to avoid this violence, it is necessary to eradicate the manifestation of violence in one's own behavior, and on a more subtle level in emotions and thoughts.

Speaking of moral and spiritual values, rules and limitations, they are all artificial and most often simply block the natural flow of vital energy. Their blind acceptance is useful in the early stages of development, until a person himself feels the natural flow of life. In this regard, development is a departure from the origins in order to gain experience, and then to return to them with an adult consciousness.

The second stage of personality development

This is the stage of the social addict - the "adapted" average citizen, for whom 90% of all television programs, magazines, games and media news are intended. Here I omit books, because for the most part they have a slightly higher level of presentation of information.

At this stage, a person intuitively feels that physical abuse must be avoided. He can bring his rationale to an understanding of why you should not behave immorally on a physical level. However, a logical explanation is not so important. What is important is deep experience in his unconscious. If you believe in rebirth, you can call it the experience of past lives, where a person worked out gross karma. Otherwise, we can talk about genes transmitted by worthy parents or about appropriate education. The physical person falls to physical violence during a regression, when his perception is temporarily dull.

However, the physical plane is not the only one. And at the second stage of development, a person can be immoral with regard to his feelings and thoughts.

At the second stage of development, for example, a person rarely understands that lying is also violence and disharmony. In other words, the problem is transferred to a more subtle - mental level. Development as such is associated with the elimination of gross misunderstanding and the shift of attention to a more subtle imbalance.

At the second stage of development, the survival instinct fades into the background, its influence becomes indirect, but gluttony and lust are still central needs. The difference with the first stage of development is that consciousness becomes an order of magnitude thinner and needs expose their shades and qualities. A person begins to play temptation and seduction in order to enjoy what is happening more sophisticatedly. In sex, there are preliminary games and affection. In food, in addition to meat and booze, there may be an interest in more refined dishes.

A characteristic feature of the second stage of development is the need for pleasure. And since the mental sphere is already to some extent developed, a person, in addition to sex and food, is interested in the delight of his mind. This includes: games, entertaining fiction, movies, chatter and all kinds of fun.

According to the criterion of wisdom and foresight, a person at the second stage of development took a noticeable step. Now he operates with memory, and is ready to earn money that he can spend on getting what he wants. At this stage, a person is prone to drug addiction and alcoholism, so the social information block condemning these inclinations is not in vain working so actively.

Another criterion of the first two stages of development is degradation in the absence of labor and vigorous activity. If a person falls into a state of the first two stages, most likely, he will soon die. An exception can only be in the case of tight control by a stronger person who is next to the person of the first two stages of development. In this case, a strong personality encloses a weaker one from indulging his passions. After all, as you know, drug addiction has a tendency to progress - whether it is a passion for games, TV, sex, alcohol, or drugs. Fortunately, a person of the second level is only rarely able to earn a lot of money. Usually he seems to maneuver between vices and his ability to quench them.

The third stage of personality development

This is the stage of the boss. It does not matter whether this person is the boss at work, in the family, or over himself, his main need is power and control. Sex, food and entertainment fade into the background, but interest in them does not fade away.

The basis for life satisfaction is manifested here as the need to change, manipulate, manage, subjugate and possess. Sexual desire at this stage of development is more manifested not at the level of lust, but more often as a moral and emotional need to "possess". For this person in a relationship, for example, it is more important to win and win. And often, when this desire is realized, he loses interest in the relationship - he won't be interested in conquering the same territory twice. An exception at this stage of development may be a craving for a person from a more subtle level. We are drawn to those whose stages of development are higher than ours, who understand life a little more subtle, who are more sensitive and responsive. As a rule, we are most drawn to the society of those people who are able to manifest one level above ours. This is due to our own perspective and unconscious need to rise to the next stage.

If two people communicate in whom the difference in the stages of development is two or more, they do not have a mutual understanding. More precisely, the advanced personality is clearly aware of the needs of the average person. All of her desires and soul movements of an advanced personality are in full view, and therefore, if there is any interest in the personality from the initial stages of development, then it is more likely to be educational or experimental in nature. A person is not capable of understanding a person from a more advanced stage of development - understanding will be limited to the framework of his own level. In the best case, a person honestly acknowledges and accepts his inability to understand, and most often falls into self-deception, believing that the scope of his mind is life.

A person of the third stage of development can join the society of people of the first and second stages of development - either on business or if he has unworked programs at these levels. However, the current level of visionary wisdom encourages him to work with his weaknesses. Such a person is able to quit smoking, or drink abruptly, simply by his willful decision - that is, a clear understanding of the consequences. At this stage of development, his personality is crystallized to some extent, and is able to methodically follow his own decisions, the understanding of which is present due to relative personal integrity.

Violence and rudeness at this stage of personality development can manifest itself as coldness in feelings, greed, refined pride and a sense of self-importance developed to the limit, forcing a person to humiliate and worry about his own person. ChSV becomes thinner and its intensity decreases significantly, starting from the fourth stage of personality development.

If a person does not have gross programs from the first two stages of personality development, he can be honest, reasonable and fair. But the refinement of his perception is not enough to understand what he really wants from life. He feels protected and satisfied when he feels control over the situation. However, in reality, this control is nothing more than a shaky illusion, from which he stubbornly hides in his affairs. Life does not obey strict logical laws. Life is a spontaneous phenomenon, and much more complex than the concepts that are available for understanding at the third stage of personality development.

The first three stages of the development of personality and consciousness constitute the social sphere of life. The next three stages, conditionally, can be called the spiritual stages of development. They will be discussed further.

Fourth stage of personality development

This is the blissful stage. The person at this stage releases his grip on the ego and self-importance. I would call this stage a true growing up, because now a person is able to truly take care of others, as if he himself had finally ceased to be a child, forever in need of patrons. A person from the first three stages is not interested in this. Even reading these lines may cause him gloom. And, on the contrary, interest in this topic suggests that the person is as if ready, he is already at the bridge from the social to the spiritual. The transition itself can be lengthy, and if you do not take conscious steps, showing conscious wisdom, the path to the fourth stage takes decades, and it may not happen.

What is the meaning and joy of living for the sake of others? What is meant by development at this level in comparison with the third stage? To understand this, you can ask yourself a different question. What is the meaning and joy of living for yourself? Are people truly happy in the early stages of development? If you exaggerate a little, then the person living for himself wants to subdue the world of his personality. Will he be happy if his wishes come true? He will be infinitely lonely. To communicate heart to heart with loved ones, you must be able to open up. When the fire of greed burns the soul, to be yourself is painful and scary. Before pouring out of the vessel of the soul, the lava of lust for power burns the body with its cold fire.

At the fourth stage of development, perception takes on a new depth, and a person becomes even more sensitive and attentive to what is happening. He sees that wisdom does not know selfishness, and the constant pulling the blankets to his side. In his foresight, he knows that hatred, lies, greed and selfishness do not lead to happiness. When it comes to fulfilling desires, it gives only a brief moment of satisfaction, then the endless race for an illusory future continues.

At the fourth stage of development, a person feels the fears and false incentives of other people (from the first to the third stage), but this does not cause sublime condemnation in him. On the contrary, he sympathizes with those who are in ignorance. If you analyze, most people in the early stages of development spend most of their time and money in vain, or even to their own detriment. A well-developed third stage of development gives a person the strength of a social level. At the fourth stage, a person gains a certain kind of wisdom in how to use this power.

I spoke in sufficient detail about this stage of development in the article "Faith and Knowledge". I'll quote a few quotes from there: "The saint is happy because he is not fixated on worrying about himself. He loves life, does not waste time on endless deliberation and reflection, which consumes 90% of the energy of the average man. We can say that the meaning of his life is in creation, in action, which turns into a blessing for those who are nearby. It is impossible to avoid suffering and emptiness when the ego defends its position and no self-giving occurs. "

Fifth Stage of Development

This is the stage of the sage. The transition from the third stage to the fourth is one of the most difficult, both in terms of experiences, and often in terms of events. Therefore, in our time there are people with good practices of the last stages, while inflating a sense of self-importance to the limit. Ideally, the stages of development are worked out one after another.

If at the third stage a person learned to manage events at the social level, then at the fifth, he learns to control his own consciousness, which leads to a certain kind of control of events at the metaphysical level.

If a person has worked well in the fourth stage, in the fifth his wisdom takes on even greater depth. Why do wars arise? Why are there diseases? Why do people suffer? It is at the fifth stage of development that wisdom reaches the limit when it contains a deep understanding of these things. The essence of life is not limited to the typical view of what is fair and what is not. The sage is aware of cause and effect. Each phenomenon does not happen by chance, but is a precious lesson that introduces a new element into the puzzle of life that complements the perception of a holistic picture of the world.

The vision of hidden processes at the fifth level of personality development occurs from deep perspectives. All mechanisms of life begin to be revealed at this level. If the transition from the third stage of development to the fourth was characterized by overcoming a sense of self-importance, passing through shame, guilt and a turning point in feelings, at the fifth level a person goes through disappointment in worldly ideals.

If the fourth level has not been fulfilled, and the person has not learned to love, what is happening at the fifth stage of development causes a sense of doom. However, now the power of discrimination, sensitivity and foresight are at an extremely high level. Therefore, the exposure of worldly illusions is followed by the exposure of spiritual illusions. Disappointment, doom, meaninglessness are the same illusions as everything else.

At this stage, a person is clearly aware of the wisdom of the evolutionary lessons through which he is destined to pass. Lust, irritation, greed, envy, guilt, doom and other experiences are given to become stronger. They stimulate consciousness, make it expand, so that a person does not dissolve in gross illusions. Heavy experiences encourage, at a subconscious level, to develop the power of perception and discrimination, so that thanks to these strong qualities of a mature consciousness, one can acquire the ability to digest and dissolve negative experiences. If the previous stages of development were well worked out, at the fifth stage of development a person is able to find the finest balance in all phenomena, at every moment of life. At this level, a person reacts to life according to the situation. He balances what is happening here and now at a very subtle level.

Sixth stage of development

This is an enlightened person. Upon transition to this stage, a cognitive shock is experienced. To say that at the same time a person is surprised, or even amazed - to say nothing. Enlightenment is the exposure of ignorance and the coming to the truth. At the level of events, a person can live a completely ordinary life, not standing out in a crowd, or in conversation, but in his soul everything is completely different. If the transition from the third stage of development to the fourth was a revolution in feelings, the transition to the sixth stage is characterized by a revolution of consciousness.

At this stage, perception reaches a peak, and a person sees everything as it is. He sees that life exists right now. He is aware of the past and the future as illusions in the mind. He sees that all the so-called events are just thoughts in which the average man sleeps. At this stage, the personality experiences total catharsis, perception closes on itself and deep self-awareness takes place. The personality begins to be perceived as an object with something even deeper, perceiving the personality from the side, standing on top of human life. The person is felt in the true light - beams of transient mental energy, which were centered, intertwined in the head, throat and heart region. At this stage of development, everything that a person knew about life is perceived as an illusion. The human world is a thought about thought.

The main characteristic features of this stage of development are the cessation of suffering, the relief and absence of any personal desires. Another characteristic feature is the awareness of life as a completely spontaneous phenomenon. An enlightened person realizes himself as a sensation of being, presence, the only quality of which is contemplation, perception. The viewer does not interfere with the process. Life happens spontaneously, by itself due to its internal energy. An article on the illusion of choice is devoted to this topic on progressman.ru.

Enlightenment is the realization of what is here and now. In this awareness, the person himself is perceived as one of the many phenomena that spontaneously arise in the presence of being. To understand what it is to a person from earlier stages of development is impossible. When familiarized with this as a theory, estimates may arise. However, all this is nothing more than thoughts that evaluate the same phenomenon at different times in different ways.

If a person from another stage of development survives the freedom of spontaneous being characteristic of an enlightened person, he will understand why he lives.

At different times, we sometimes jump to advanced levels and understand everything, then we go down and lose this understanding. This is due to unprocessed programs from previous stages of development. The development process itself is a central, most important aspect of human life. Therefore, the transition from one stage to another is an "event" of the greatest importance, an event with which no material goods can be compared.

Self-development through awareness and self-affirmation

Science says that egoism was formed in the mind as a property necessary for the survival of the individual. That is, egoism is such a set of measures for survival. What, then, is the ego?

All these subtle matters are so vague! So, let's say I say "spoon", then I take this spoon and put it in a mug. Everything is simple and clear. But this simplicity is ascertained by my mind. And in the mind, everything is vague and multifaceted. Mind, consciousness, subconsciousness, ego - all these are very conventional ways to at least somehow identify and explain what is happening on a "subtle", mental level.

I respect psychology, and I am anxious about some oriental teachings, which, from my point of view, speak most adequately in words about what the psyche is and how it works. For several years I was engaged in a "special" technique of contemplating my own "I". Many articles on progressman.ru appeared as a result of the information that was obtained using this particular technique. And now, when I write "I", or "ego", I can no longer mean exactly what was meant by this word, well, say, Sigmund Freud. And somehow I do not want to invent new words. So you have to get out, layering the subjective on the "generally accepted".

As a result, I sometimes sometimes hardly imagine what Freud meant when talking about the ego, because my subjective experience is more real for me than other people's words. And the more I have this experience, the oddly enough less and less specificity remains. There are more and more questions. But the search for answers no longer worries so much, because the mind began to guess: in fact, nothing to understand!

Self-development through awareness

So, what does my "I" think of itself? "I" is not a body or consciousness. "I" is the "point" where all thoughts that evaluate reality are centered. The stronger and livelier the score, the more solid a brick it becomes in the body of the "I". All these are thoughts that express an attitude towards life. To relate to something in some way means continuous self-regeneration of the "I".

From one second to another, the "I" is transferred without critical mental "losses", when it maintains a whole set of assessments about the ongoing life. The "I" seeks to maintain the evaluation-relations as particles of its own structure. The destruction of the ratings that make up the self leads to suffering.

Fear as a great suffering arises from the destruction of the structure of "I". But just such an incomplete destruction of the "I" can become the strongest catalyst for self-healing and evolution of the "I" on a more subtle level.

Freed from rough estimates (particles of its structure), the "I" replaces them with more refined and adapted to survive at a new level of self-awareness. The higher the level of self-awareness, the more actively consciousness manifests itself in mental processes, the more actively all the delusions of the mind dissolve. Awareness, as it were, reveals the structure of the next thought-assessment, and recognizes it as an illusion.

A new level of awareness kills the current level of "I" so that the "I" is reborn more refined, strong and adapted to this level of awareness. This is a painful, but very fast way to self-development.

When you feel the fifth point, what promises a new level of consciousness, you are somehow in no hurry to evolve. Everything happens in a hurry, step by step, without running ahead of the steam locomotive, "with the arrangement" ... But you no longer see any other way out. Self-development is the only true way. And there are many paths.

Surprise

But there are some "bonuses" in this business. Self-development is the most interesting activity in the world! We all know that the most amazing things are miracles. My experience suggests that surprise happens when I accept and become aware of myself on a new level. Surprise is the next layer of revealing one's own "I" and awareness of reality through it. In the limit, it causes intense amazement.

Disclosure of new layers of "I" kills the former, highlights them as illusions. And this, as mentioned above, is a painful process. Therefore, the rush here is inappropriate. At a new level, we must have time to integrate with new experience, gain new support. Otherwise, if you make it too "high", you can inadvertently enlighten, at the same time breaking up with the body.

Therefore, I do not recommend the use of psychotropic substances. They expand consciousness, open a window into the unknown of the **unconscious**, but the mind is not ready to digest information from there. So sometimes they go crazy.

Therefore, from the outset, you should not bind yourself too much with evaluations and concepts so that parting with them is not so painful. Even Sri Aurobindo said that "indisputable dogmas are the most dangerous varieties of lies."

All that we know is only temporary support of the current stage of development. Clinging to our knowledge, we assert ourselves, entertain our pride. Parting with evaluations and concepts, we free consciousness for knowledge of a new order.

Self-development through self-affirmation.

It seems that the contradiction is in our blood. On the one hand, the ego clings to estimates and stops, on the other, it seeks to develop. But why does our ego need self-development? Why get out of a cozy swamp comfort zone? The ego is simply dragging itself away from the perspectives that loom at new stages of development.

The ego potentially feels that it can become strong and advanced. And becoming stronger, he will be able to assert himself much more skillfully! Egoism is a powerful motivator of self-development.

Our mind is a surprisingly arrogant contraption! It is a collection of concepts about what is happening in life. But the mind itself, at times, believes that it is a set of laws by which life lives.

Subjective concepts of the mind differ from the "objective" laws of reality, just as fantasy differs from a living person. In the mind, everything mixes up and becomes fantasies, because the mind itself is capable of operating only with concepts, but not with the real laws of being.

Self-affirmation as a motive for self-development, encourages efficiency and success. To do this, we use awareness - as it develops, our concepts of life become more and more realistic. The more the concepts of the mind are like reality, the more effective you become by putting them into practice. Honest realism is the key to personal effectiveness.

Awareness rips off our masks, removes support from the ego, destroys stereotypes, exposes illusions and attachments. But, in my opinion, it's much more interesting to see real miracles than to be content with "secrets" that are kept on lies. That is how yesterday's gross tendencies of the mind "burn". And somewhere around here, all the frames begin to blur.

It's probably not so important that it directs our self-development. Somewhere - selfishness, fear and self-affirmation, somewhere - morality, guilt, courage and valor, and somewhere - a craving for an unknown, transcendent, amazing reality outside of concepts.

Levels of development of consciousness

Levels of development of consciousness in this article are considered through the prism of instincts, intelligence and intuition. This classification of levels of development can be used as a global ladder of evolution on the planet, but here it is used to consider specifically human evolution. Social, psychological and spiritual aspects of personality development are discussed in more detail in the article "stages of personality development". And here I continue the topic of "decision-making" - this is the topic of influences - causes and motives that encourage us to act under the guidance of instincts, intelligence and intuition.

Each person, **depending on the level of development of consciousness,** has various types of incentives, reasons for committing certain actions, and in general for making decisions and choosing as such. Below I will briefly describe the varieties of basic incentives.

Animal (instinctive) level of consciousness development

Instincts are reactions aimed at satisfying basic bodily needs. Animals as creatures, not yet capable of reasonable conclusions and actions, are forced to experience almost constant fear in order to avoid dangers: to run away, smelling the smell of a predator, to seek food and shelter. Animals at their **level of development** have an excellent response since Do not spend time analyzing and considering the situation. Their actions can be called absolutely sincere, direct. Animals act instantly, according to the situation, but their reaction is limited by a blurred shallow instinctive level of consciousness.

The human (intellectual) level of development of consciousness.

Intellect means awareness of the goal on the mental level, logical understanding and the choice of the best way to implement it. For a person as a creature of a more intelligent, fear no longer plays such a significant role, because for most of the work of the psyche, for decision-making, intelligence is now responsible. Fear shines somewhere at the subconscious level. Nevertheless, the average man is still far from absolute rationality, and if we assume at his **level of development of consciousness the** possibility of the complete elimination of fear, this unreasonableness will fully manifest itself - a person will begin to commit reckless and life-threatening acts. This is clearly manifested in behavior under the influence of alcohol, when feelings are dulled due to a narrowing of consciousness.

In other words, in a sphere where the mind does not manifest itself to its full potential, tougher control organs come to the scene, associated with the manifestation of the evolutionary past (animal level of development of consciousness). And here I make one bold assumption: when a person brings absolute rationality into action, fear and rude emotions go away forever.

The physical reaction at the human level of development of consciousness in comparison with the animal level is inhibited, because a person perceives reality through a layer of mental buffer in which an assessment and analysis of the situation takes place. Depending on the level of rationality (the power of discernment), a person, in the course of analysis, makes the right or wrong decisions resulting in relatively effective actions.

The development of consciousness on a human level is possible only in a state of imbalance, when there is a problem, when the present does not satisfy and there is something to strive for. And the state of "satisfaction" in most cases not only stops the development of consciousness at the current level, but also leads to degradation.

You may have heard about a famous experiment where scientists connected electrodes to the mouse brain and made a special pedal, clicking on which the mouse experienced an orgasm. After several hundred orgasms experienced within an hour, the mouse died of energy loss. In other words, at a certain level of development in conditions of continuous bliss, a living organism comes to degradation and extinction.

The question arises: can a person develop without suffering? It turns out that on the human level of development, consciousness is forced to experience discomfort only for the reason that happiness without suffering ultimately leads to extinction. Unfortunately, at the current level of development of our society, paradoxically, a person is forced to be in relative danger in order to survive.

To understand the true causes of human misfortune, it is necessary to analyze our current level of development of consciousness, the nature of our self-identification. For a layman, reality looks like a kind of serious strategic game. In this game we have a personal layout of cards. Among the weak cards: our vulnerabilities, fears and debts. Among the trump cards: abilities, resources, communications. We use the existing alignment to achieve the desired goals, overcoming weaknesses. All this is the external, superficial side of the human level of development of consciousness. The inner side is immeasurably more complicated - it boils with countless experiences, feelings, thoughts, many unconscious influences.

Human intelligence is a kind of psychic magnet with the polarities of plus and minus, good and bad, good and evil. Intelligence is designed in such a way that a person is drawn to pleasant experiences, and repels unpleasant ones. It is the intellect that divides reality into dual spectra: happiness and suffering, good and evil, light and dark, high and low, etc. And as long as we identify with the intellect, for us the principle of its work is dominant. Suffering on the human level of development of consciousness is inevitable. And all the wisdom is to live with dignity the required portion of complex experiences - without suppression and looping - with the least resistance.

In favorable conditions, in any paradise for a dual mind, any incentives for further actions cease to exist, because everything suits, and consciousness at the human level of development in comfort inevitably falls asleep, slides to a grosser, more animal level - below the threshold of vibration of intelligence.

Therefore, those small obstacles and the discomfort that life suits us can be perceived as grace, as the most effective method of developing consciousness at its current level of evolution. In paradise, the layman becomes dumber and degrades, in everyday life and in work - it grows and develops.

The experiences of our world are dual. Being attached to pleasant experiences, we inevitably experience suffering. On the one hand, such duality looks unfair. Is it really impossible without suffering at the human level of development? On the other hand, if a person experienced only pleasant experiences, he would not have incentives for further movement, he could not leave his current level, for the sake of a more subtle one, and would forever remain in dumb oblivion. Suffering is an instrument of development.

A pleasant state is just a particle of truth, pain is its opposite, which seems to tell us to wake up, leave this "half-truth", release these images, illusions, and move to new levels of development of consciousness - to truth and freedom. Therefore, conscious, intentional evolution is so important when you are moving not from under a stick, but by the power of your own understanding.

Perhaps nature itself is intended for us to know the essence of what is happening, to go beyond our own mind to a higher level of development of consciousness; and only then can the thirst for the unity of opposites, for harmony and integrity, be truly satisfied.

Intuitive level of development of consciousness

In the course of development, consciousness gradually begins to consider the plane of intelligence as deeply secondary, and ceases to be absorbed in thoughts. Intelligence is an extremely effective factor in the evolution of nature, that transient link (level of development), due to which consciousness interacts with the world of objects, makes us, being in instability, constantly move to a new level of comfort. But, like any system, the mental mechanism someday begins to exhaust itself, reaches its limit, and under certain conditions gives way to new, more subtle and effective tools of cognition.

In the course of observing what was happening, I developed a peculiar esoteric concept - I do not advise taking on faith, but it makes sense to observe its manifestation in my life. The fact is that nature requires human growth and self-knowledge (constant transition to new levels of development), and when this happens intentionally, consciously, then forces from above reduce the number of gross "karmic" events - troubles that encourage one to grow above oneself due to negative experiences. In other words, even though a person is influenced by the "law" of the carrot and stick, he can consciously choose the "carrot", then the "blows" of the carrot are no longer necessary. With a conscious approach, the working out of karma and the release of stresses occur more smoothly than in cases when a person does not understand the cause of the events and experiences that arise.

At the human level of development of consciousness, we are inclined to look for the cause of internal experiences in the external world, which is fundamentally wrong, because the outside world carries only the appearance of this reason. On this topic on progressman.ru there are a number of articles under the tag "projection". Events actually line themselves up in accordance with that karma, with those experiences for which it is time to manifest themselves at the current level of development of consciousness. The event level in a sense in general is illusory because without our thoughts and feelings he does not have a "coloring", of any significance. In fact, nothing exists outside the limits of thought, and there has never been, except one ... Outside of the mind, there is only one event and this event is God. Depending on faith, or intellectual preferences, the word "God" can be replaced, for example: by absolute, unmanifest reality, impersonal chaos, paradoxical objective eternal "now". This truth becomes apparent at the intuitive level of development of consciousness.

In the context of these circumstances, the meaning of every person's life is in the development of consciousness. When a person truly reaches the stage of reason, he gains the opportunity to go beyond it - beyond the boundaries of the dual world, in which everything was divided into different aspects of the pleasant and the unpleasant.

At a deeper level of development of consciousness, the mind shares its role with intuition, eventually completely giving way to the reins of government. Intuition manifests itself as a factor of confidence in the reality. There is a feeling of absolute spontaneity of what is happening. You are in the "center" of existence, as if all reality revolves around you. Your nature is pure existence, a formless spectator of life. At this level of development of consciousness, the mental buffer is eliminated, and a spontaneous reaction to each impulse follows immediately. From this level, the experience begins, referred to in the Eastern teachings by the term "lila" - a spontaneous game.

So, we can distinguish three levels of development of consciousness and three levels of stimuli that guide our behavior: animal, human and divine. Or in other words: instinctive, intellectual and intuitive levels. Instinct - following a reflex in order to achieve a goal that is not even fully understood. Intelligence implies awareness of the goal on a mental level, logical understanding and the choice of the best path to it. Intuition is the essential, true awareness of the goal and the path. "Intuitio" from Latin is translated as contemplation. To see the truth outside the mind, awareness is needed. Intuition is the ability to soberly assess the situation with direct consciousness, bypassing the mental buffer.

The main message that this article is intended to give on three levels of development of consciousness is the understanding, at least at the level of the mind, that continuous development and self-knowledge is the true goal of our stay in the current conditions of life.

The quirks of the unconscious

Why do even materialists deep down believe in a higher power?

Why even in a happy marriage do we look at others?

Why do you worry about breaking up with a loved one more than once, but many?

Why is outdoor activity satisfying?

It may seem to you that these issues are not related. In fact, they point to the same phenomenon.

Imagine a multi-storey building where a mysterious many-sided creature lives. On each floor - his new hypostasis. On the lower side is its ancient incomprehensible essence. On the next is his animal manifestation. Above, it is a baby in the human body. Even higher is the child. Then a teenager. On the top floor you find yourself.

Our psyche resembles a constantly under construction house. We are well acquainted with the upper floor: our everyday self lives here. We barely see the floor below - it borders on our unconscious. The deeper the floor, the more difficult it is to perceive. The lower floors are buried in the abyss of the unconscious.

We perceive life on all floors at the same time. Without noticing it. We may not suspect how deep down we are worried about something. From the lower floors only vague moods reach the surface.

What does this stratification of the psyche lead to? I will tell you with examples.

It comes gradually

When we part with relatives, for example, in a divorce, we experience separation not once, but many. Until it reaches every floor of the psyche. Therefore, it is so easy to part - and it is so difficult to endure a separation.

At first, the superficial "I" says goodbye with naive ease. The next day it reaches the floor below - and the pain of loss covers with unexpected strength: I want to return the spouse and forgive him everything. And this is not the last goodbye.

After years, when everything has long been forgotten, once in a dream, feelings suddenly return, and you say goodbye again. This means - awareness has reached the depths of the unconscious.

At this level, maximum tragedy. The pain of loss burns the bare nerves of the soul. But passes in a minute.

You may be surprised for the first time in years: how strange and wrong it is to lose your very own person. It's like they just broke up. He was a native in the past. But the unconscious does not reflect in what time life flows. There, in the bowels of the soul, the former spouse is still the main person in life.

Also with former friends. You do not communicate for years. And in a dream, still be friends.

God is a projection of parents

Have you ever wondered what it means to believe in God? How do we know what God is? What do we really believe in? To whom do we offer prayers?

Imagine that you are still a year old. The majestic figure of mother rises above you. And above it is light ... - a light from the ceiling. You do not have clear thoughts yet. But you feel - this creature is powerful and most important. Your life depends on him. And this feeling is imprinted in memory forever.

Then you grow up, you see that mom is a person like you. But the children's perception of a higher being above you does not go away, but remains in the unconscious. And you live on with this vague feeling: the majestic, caring and punishing parent is somewhere nearby. Now you think that it is God.

It is worth crying - and God will regret. And if God does not love, it is like death.

If you were beaten in childhood, you think that God is strict and can severely punish. That way you can live your whole life in fear. If you were spoiled in childhood, you can believe that you are also a favorite of God.

I do not claim that religiosity is caused by neuroses alone. I already raised this topic on progressman.ru in the article "Religion of the Neurotic".

The ancient world

Our ancient unconscious has not yet been rebuilt under the modern world. For the depths of the unconscious - we are still in the Stone Age, in caves.

When you return home to warmth after activity in the fresh air, you feel satisfaction. For the unconscious, you have just returned from a successful hunt.

In the ancient world, sitting in four walls meant slow death. Therefore, retreat is good soil for the spleen. The unconscious does not reflect that today you can succeed without protruding from the cave. If wifi is connected to it.

In the Stone Age, to get out of the collective and become an outcast was death. Therefore, we are still in the old habit of so important someone else's opinion. Any hint of a low position in the flock is like a death warrant. The unconscious does not reflect that today you can be a thriving sociophobe.

Internal conflicts

The unconscious constantly wedges itself into our daily life without demand. These are intuitive guesses, insights, unexpected impulses. But more often uninvited emotions make their way from there.

Do you want to be collected and strong-willed? You have wild, unbridled desires. Want to be decent and balanced? Catch the anger! He took an oath? And the unconscious in the know?

The unconscious does not know the rules of modern society. We constantly restrain the ancient man.

The unconscious does not believe in monogamy - and can tire out the forbidden attraction. Take for example a man who loves his wife and is faithful to her. He will still be interested in other women - and may sneak a peek at them sneakily.

Here lies the most interesting. If such a decent man realizes why he is turning his neck to beauties, then he will be surprised to find that he is trying on them, as it were: a new intimacy, new feelings ...

Do you notice a contradiction? Not going to change, but considering options. Without realizing it.

When a man looks at other women, he forgets for a moment that he has a wife. Forcing her into the unconscious. Some small part of his inside peers into the women - a subpersonality from another floor of the soul. She has her own goals. She doesn't even know that a man has a wife. Wife in another memory location.

After two seconds, the man, as it were, regains consciousness and upsets himself. His conscious comes into conflict with the unconscious.

Most of all our problems are due to lack of integrity. Our gut is an empire of conflicting authorities. Therefore, it is so difficult to be true to your decisions. Therefore, it is so difficult to achieve sustainable self-esteem and self-confidence. Therefore, it is so difficult to accept and love yourself. There are too many things mixed up in us.

Do not be afraid of your unexpected emotions and do not close yourself from them. Recognize your experiences. Otherwise, muffled pain persists for years. Depression is a good example of suppressed fear.

The less psyche has protective layers, the more intense is the emotion: it burns harder and more quickly exhausts itself. As a result, you clear yourself and calm comes.

Exercise, walk in the fresh air. This is both beneficial and uplifting.

We love gifts and holidays, because we so please our inner child. Children playing and rejoicing connect us, as it were, to childhood - and the world again seems magical.

Such miniature schizophrenia is an everyday occurrence; it happens to everyone. But if the internal schism grows, then conflicting desires tear the soul to pieces. So there are already large-scale mental disorders.

On the top floor - you are current, relevant. On the floor below - you are five years old. Even lower is the child. And the very first floor is your ancient evolutionary past.

Every year we finish building a new floor - and a new "I" arises on it - the one you feel now. Our "I" from the past do not disappear completely, but remain in the unconscious. They pop up when the situation turns them on, in a dream, when there is not enough energy, for example, during an illness.

How is development going?

We are all surprisingly blind to ourselves. On the machine we speak and don't hear our words, intonations, we don't feel facial expressions. And the saddest thing is that we don't understand what exactly and why we are doing it - we don't realize our motives. As if we were not acting, but something alien through us. And on the surface there remains a helpless mask, grimacing under the onslaught of automatisms. And after all, just about everyone lives this way, without even realizing it.

We simply do not see ourselves. And without seeing our motives, we time ourselves and others about the reasons for our actions.

What and what are you doing here and now?

Each attentive look affects itself. When you see yourself, you cannot remain the same. Not because he arrogantly decided to change. But because the magic of oblivion is dispelled.

What motives do you serve?

Have you ever thought about how to grow up? How are you developing?

I remember in my childhood I saw layers falling from my personality. Of course, I did not really understand what was happening. He just noticed how inclinations change.

At first, you disappointedly catch yourself in repetitive reactions. You begin to realize how "do not." You come to a standstill. Then new feelings come, new words. You become a different person.

We never see what is leading us. Only vaguely feel. Some unclear motives … And when we begin to realize them, the motives immediately change to the next stage of invisibility. Flat out.

So we grow up. Redefine ourselves. Again and again. Layer by layer.

Recently, one of my clients suddenly realized that it turned out that she had avenged her whole life. Not noticing it myself. For years, the same situation repeated under her nose. As if with lateral vision through the thickness of sleep, she dimly caught what was happening. But year after year she continued to obey blind automatisms. Until I realized myself clearer.

When vague motives become apparent, they dissipate like a dream. So you can change dramatically in a short time.

The child boasts with touching spontaneity. Adults give feedback, and the child notices his little trick.

To once again catch yourself in self-deception, you will need the next level of awareness. It may take years. When the elders smile at the behavior of a teenager, he periodically looks at himself - and realizes ...

When you grow up, the motives become thin again. Now you don't brag like a child, don't bend your fingers like a teenager, but emphasize your importance as if by chance: smart phrases, sense of humor, "involuntary" mention of your achievements. "Modest but tasteful."

As before, without really understanding what and why you are doing ...

Such motives as if the partisans on enemy territory after the lost battle do not give up, but hide until the last, in order to stealthily take their own.

During the course of my life I myself was aware of dozens of my inclinations. He was touchy and boring, threw off responsibility, did not understand that sometimes I demand the impossible from life. I feel that now I am deceiving myself on many issues. Everything, like everyone else.

A dim light

We never see our self-deception. We can only vaguely guess about it. As soon as it is opened to appear before our gaze, it immediately dissipates - as if it were not.

We are the vehicles of invisible influences. We don't really see ourselves, we don't realize what we really believe in. We think and act out of habit.

Imagine a moth flying blindly toward the light. What reality is it in? He is neither aware of himself nor the reasons for his movement through the air. Light scorches his wings. The moth is dying.

This is an analogy of human life.

Do we understand what and why we are doing? Do we understand who we are? Or blindly rushing under the influence of vague sensations to a dim light?

Choice is an illusion, a boundary between those who have power and those who do not. Take a look at this woman. God, just look at her. She is so plain, gray. But he is trying to change the whole world for himself! Look - here I sent her something for dessert. This is a very unusual dessert. I created this program. It starts very simply. But each subsequent line of the program causes all new reactions. Like poetry. At first she blushes. She gets hot, her heart beats more and more. She does not know what is going on. Maybe it's because of the wine? No. What is this? What is the reason? But it soon becomes irrelevant. Soon she forgets that there was some reason. She is worried about sensations. Consequence This is the nature of the universe. We deny it, try to fight. But all this is only a pretense and a lie! Behind our comfort is the truth: we have absolutely no control over our lives. Have not learned yet!

Disagreements with reality

Our psyche scans reality, makes its miniature casts in the mind, then reacts to them. That's how we live.

You swim through life in a half-trance. Then, some kind of hindrance to the material world interrupts your sleep. There is a "template break", and you are indignantly surprised. It turns out that reality has disagreements with you!

Clash with the unknown expands consciousness, makes you look at yourself and your life from the side.

We grow up when we discard obsolete patterns of thinking, and begin to become aware of life more accurately and in detail. Layer by layer, the coarse casts of reality in our mind die off. They are replaced by new, refined ones.

The onion of our personality consists of layers of dreams. It is worth focusing on the mirage, as it immediately dissipates. We grow up when we re-realize ourselves.

Again and again. Layer by layer.

Awareness and oblivion

When you are immersed in an emotional trance, you do not understand what you are doing and why. You become a blind conductor of automatisms.

If you hurt a loved one out of habit, and suddenly on the go you realize this, this is the most amazing moment when you change before your eyes. You look at your motives from the side: yesterday I took them for granted; today they are not exciting.

An attentive reader could notice the main leitmotif of the latest articles on progressman.ru. This is a call to realize where you are moving in the stream of life, what choices you make here and now.

Ask yourself:

What am I doing with my life right now?

What will my words and actions lead to?

What motives do I serve?

Who am I feeling?

What do I believe in?

Ask for real. Give each question time. Look into yourself.

The more awareness, the more sensitive and accurate you react to the moment of life.

In oblivion you act automatically, reactions are clumsy and rude. In awareness, every moment is honored with your individual approach.

We begin to understand each other when we hear ourselves, our tone, our words. When we hear the interlocutor, we are aware of the meanings of his words and gestures.

You can spend your whole life on your thoughts and feelings. And you can look at them. To study them. You yourself are the main object of your own research.

Many people are familiar with the situation when you perceive the oldest person over the years as the youngest. It was as if he had not matured, but had only grown old. You see his reactions and feel - you have passed it. A long time ago.

But it happens, you realize - in something, a person is more complex and deeper than you, but in something, like a child. For example, she thinks faster and more logically, but feels like you ... ten years ago.

So we complement each other with strengths. And it strengthens the relationship.

When you no longer know what to do and what to do, it seems that you have reached a dead end. In fact, you are the only way out of it. Rise above habitual patterns of thinking. They don't have you anymore. And in this silence of the mind new intuitive solutions are born ...

The main lesson that we all go through is naivety. We are developing, by grinding our thinking with life. Reality ruthlessly destroys illusions. You look around more and more, as if you had just been born.

The world of adult children

As a psychologist, after meeting heart to heart with many adults, I know for sure - we are not sure. There are only those who skillfully disguise themselves, depicting the confidence demanded by today's stereotypes, convincing in its reality not only those around them, but also themselves. Tomorrow stereotypes will change, and will portray something else.

There are no truly adults among us. Women seek their fathers to hide behind them, like behind a stone wall from an incomprehensible, terrible life. For the same purpose, men, not realizing themselves, dream of mummies, in order to hide with their heels from a misunderstanding of what, in general, to do with their lives.

Nobody really understands life. But deep down, and sometimes even clearly, everyone is sure of his unique helplessness, as if he alone is afraid of life, and the rest understand everything, live in an adult world where everyone understands itself. Everything is "clear" to everyone.

Everyone in this "understandable" world is like an impostor, who really doesn't understand anything at all. But to pierce and betray your insecurity means to show that you are not mature enough to this world, that you are abnormal, underdeveloped.

Almost no one understands that mentally adults are not among us. Therefore, everyone is shaking over his personal insecurity, as if over secret leprosy, which, by all means, must be hidden from everyone. Almost everyone implicitly believes that he is such a helpless coward - alone, and the rest live in an adult world that you need to be able to reach out to show that you are worthy of him.

But we are not ready to admit our insecurity and helplessness, because we continue to blindly believe in the fictitious world of worthy, self-confident, adult people, who are supposed to somehow fit in. And then everything will be "OK."

Imagine a drunkard who, trying to show how handsome he is, is dancing. But instead of graceful and dexterous movements, absurd, clubfoot antics come out of him. In the same way, in our attempts to reach the standards of the "adult" world, we begin to grimace and draw, imagining how to break the applause.

That exultant type of self-confidence, which a person usually hunts for, can truly be achieved, probably, by some immortal deities, whose supports of movement in reality are eternal and indestructible. We, mere mortals, can only temporarily imitate that ideal, divine splendor, reveling in self-confidence while the "card is coming".

The real certainty of a mere mortal, as it can be, is agreement with the facts. At heart, we are all frightened children who find themselves at the crossroads of two roads - chaos and suspense. Some of us feel a little older, but remain children.

"Real" development

Poppy psychological literature has a weakness for rustic slogan tips. "Love yourself!" - This, one of the most popular, we have recently discussed. He has a fellow: "Be yourself!" - the same dubious and simple-minded, if you try to swallow it as it is, without understanding the contents of the subject.

What does it mean to be yourself? Aren't we already ourselves? Usually, this phrase is understood as a vague call to follow one's own heart, to embody one's unique personal potential, not to change oneself, bending to the expectations of others. All this is wonderful. But does not work. But it doesn't work because they are not rushing towards the true self, but towards the desired self. Therefore, as usual, instead of studying and understanding themselves, they are trying to improve themselves. And here it would be necessary to honestly admit that you don't really know anything about yourself, and therefore ideas about how you should be in your true appearance are all fantasies that do not lead anywhere beyond emotional impulses.

Shock development

We can say that there are two ways to develop and know yourself. The first is ostentatious. The second is real, practical.

Showy development is the most common. It is used, in simple terms, to cheer yourself up with an interesting, inspiring hobby. It is practiced by a comprehensive familiarization with the outside of the case - reading literature, watching videos, visiting practicing groups, talking with teachers and associates.

This practice of information storage is usually called development. It seems like, the more "advanced" theories in your head, the higher your own "level".

By means of ostentatious development, a person is not so much developing as trying to show it to himself - to convince himself that there is a real path and that he is moving along this path. For this purpose, the mind, which needs such visible evidence of development, feeds itself with its external attributes. When the appearance of involvement in the path is formed, the mind rejoices in the acquired meaning - the ephemeral supports of its future well-being.

This is somewhat similar to role-playing games, where participants, dressing in the costumes of fairy-tale characters, expect to thus be in a real fairy tale.

For the same purpose, popular memes are also used on social networks - thematic posters with fashionable quotes and slogans. Memes are not so much a source of useful information as decorative decoration of a virtual showcase of personal fetishes, with which the ego of the page owner covers himself.

"Real" development

As for real mental development, one can catch up with drama and say that it does not exist, in general. Sounds outrageous, huh? But for a person, by virtue of its nature, everything is ostentatious. It in itself is a kind of external frame of truth, which in its wild simplicity is far from social ideals.

We will probably talk in more detail about what the "face of truth" is next time.

And it can be said that real development is still possible, but it is played out not there and not in the way a superficial personality seems to be. We are looking for him in the midst of external paraphernalia - teachers, parties, seminars, books, ritual devices - and there is nothing wrong with that. Thus the mind receives the desired meanings.

But a real shift happens almost always unexpectedly in isolation from the outside fuss at such moments when attention suddenly turns to that area of the inside, which hitherto avoided.

At the mental level, we consist of knowledge - of our own beliefs about life. When we recognize ourselves and become "deeper," our mental structure in our own eyes becomes increasingly clear, so that the true is strengthened and the false is scattered. This process of self-clarification really resembles a well-known metaphor, where the dust of ignorance is erased from the surface of the mirror of consciousness.

And all this happens at such a deep level that the superficial person with his outward demonstrative development at best guesses, fleetingly touching, and more often does not suspect. A person with his truth is an image, a walking advertisement of his own unknown inside.

Therefore, real practice, whatever it may be, whether it is introspection, awareness, or some kind of bioenergy, has nothing to do with the halo that is being built around it. In its simplicity fresh to the mind, it is more like brushing your teeth, or washing dishes.

And that growth of personality, which, as usual, is counted on, is something implied - something that is really not here and now, but somewhere in the coming "tomorrow" it is arrogantly looking forward to.

"The changes outlined by the surface mind are sometimes fabulously far from actual possibilities. "A person cannot measure his real potential, and even more so, he is not able to predict the insights and shocks necessary for mental development."

We cannot improve ourselves in the desired direction that ostentatious spiritual development is aiming at. And a serious, prudent approach in this matter is self-seduction. In reality, we can only play development without any mandatory goals, and at the same time win something unexpectedly. Without bars and ranks, we can feel for interest in that simple process that happens in the present.

Depression: symptoms and treatment

In depression, you are like in an endless nightmare swim - it's worth relaxing and going down immediately. And the coast is not visible. Only vague hope and fear of death make us move with all our might.

Symptoms of depression: endless dull pain, conviction of the meaninglessness of life and chronic fatigue.

Imagine that you are busy with a business that you do not like. You will quickly lose energy. Even a boring movie can tire you. In depression, you live like this day after day. And it can last for years. This is a state of extortion. You get tired of everything quickly, because you do everything not out of love, but through "I don't want to".

And the most insidious feature of depression is the terrifying belief that it will never end. Because of this, hands fall. Why live if it always will be? Therefore, suicidal thoughts in depression are commonplace.

Depression is suppressed fear

One of the definitions I give for depression is suppressed fear.

Fear is the keenest emotion. It is so unpleasant that the psyche displaces it. She has such a protective mechanism - she puts intolerable experiences into the unconscious. Just hiding them from himself. But in the unconscious, they do not disappear, but continue to live an independent life. And this fear, suppressed in the depths of the soul, is depression. He continues to sound a dull pain. She is a taste of depression.

The revealed fear has the property of burning out in minutes, rarely hours. If significant supports are threatened, as in war, fear can last up to several days. Then it decays and leaves for a long time.

And suppressed fear can last for years. You really don't feel it. Muffled pain remains - the main symptom of depression. Her psyche can turn even her whole life ...

Therefore, the first key to overcoming depression is the return of fear. No matter how strange it sounds: do not be afraid of your fears!

By suppressing fear, you lose a whole layer of the soul, where desires and vital energy remain. Therefore, when you reveal your fear, desires slowly return, and with them the taste for life.

Another symptom of depression is self-estrangement

 Our worldview has this property - to pretend to be a life "in general." That is, we take our ideas about the real as reality itself. What does this lead to? Personal boundaries seem to be the boundaries of the whole universe; small personal dreams seem the only chance in the whole universe for happiness.

Therefore, in the next lover you grab hold of a dead grip. Without it, life is "empty" and "meaningless." A popular fallacy. Depressed often fail from a failed relationship.

Life is infinite. There are billions of people. How do we know that only one holds the key to our happiness?

But we presumptuously accept our tiny ghostly worldview for the whole world. And in this bouquet of mirages we seek illusory happiness and call it the only one in the whole world. Therefore, parting with a beloved is revered for the death of happiness. So our mind is deceiving itself.

We do not know all life. For life, we take a tight track, fenced by our fears. Such is the infinity compressed to the size of an apartment. And beyond it is empty space. So take your fears for the walls of the world.

How does fear limit? For example, there is a dream. I want to translate it. But unusual routes are scary. You start thinking about it and fear repels. It feels like an invisible wall in front of you. Fear from her dares - and you no longer understand what you are afraid of. So you lose contact with your fear and along with desire. Separating from a particle of your soul.

Therefore, most people do not realize how many interesting things there are in the world that they are just scared to achieve.

Another symptom of depression - the hopelessness

Desire - is the energy of the individual. Desires charge, give strength to move. If you are not an enlightened Buddha, a desireless, purposeless life will seem like a tragic path to nowhere. No strength to step into such a future remains.

Therefore, depression is not only that the soul hurts, but also constant fatigue. Everything - through "I do not want". You feel as if you are slipping into a dark hole, where, as a result, they will bury it.

Forces always stand out as desired. Therefore, it is important to establish contact with your desires. In no case do not depreciate them, do not suppress. Desires illuminate the path of life.

It may seem that desire is a fragile shield from the all-embracing depressing meaninglessness of life. They say that you need to find and catch meanings, and depression is a natural state: always behind you, stalks, and you should stumble, lose relationships, meaningful acquaintances, work - and it will absorb.

And this is an illusion.

In fact, depression is not natural. She is a belief in a negative future. It is terrible to be in an empty, meaningless life, devoid of the light of happiness.

Losing faith in the future is the most insidious symptom of depression.

No matter how difficult the situation may be, if I am sure that tomorrow, in a month, or even a year, happiness will return, then there will be no depression. Sometimes you just don't notice what you believe in, how you look forward to tomorrow.

Even a teenager can lose faith in the future. It will seem to him that he has recognized the universe - everything is perishable and in vain being. There is nothing to catch - this is the terrifying "truth of life" by default.

And of course, this is not the truth of life. This is the truth of his limited track. He understood everything about his comfort zone, played enough of his children's games. The time has come for new "games." But he is scared to move on. And from fear, life narrows to the usual rut - it confuses the easily accessible with the whole universe.

When it seems as if you knew everything and it makes you sad, remember that there are people who are much wiser. And they spin from life. They live interestingly.

Correct Desires

Spiritual seekers may be indignant at my calls to protect their desires, because the Buddha himself instructed them to drop them — all torment from them.

At progressman.ru, I have already said that there are two types of desires. The first are painful expectations. From them really continuous torment. And there is a variety of desires that make life interesting.

In the morning I prefer to drink hot water with honey, I prefer a good ecology and mild climate, I prefer a company of sensitive and informed people. But if I start to demand all this from life in the format "God forbid it doesn't work out", my happiness becomes dependent on specific conditions. Without any warranty.

Do not expect anything. Prefer. This is the secret.

Expectations poison life. While you wait, you do not live here and now, but avoid the present moment, rushing towards an imaginary future.

Almost all spiritual and psychological practices come down to **accepting the present**. Let me remind you that depression is an illusion - faith in a dark future. If you are able to live here and now, you really do not need any desires.

It is important to understand that freedom from the desires of an enlightened Buddha is not the same as deafness to one's desires in depression.

In depression, you suppress your desires. They continue to sound deep down and hurt. But in an enlightened state there is no desire, because you are already in the very epicenter of life, in the treasured "here and now".

Therefore, do not be fooled by abstract nirvana. Saying everything worldly is senseless fuss for sheep from a social herd. Such an approach devalues desires: to achieve them is simply scary - it is easier to call meaningless - they say, all the fuss is vanity and the languor of the spirit. This is a shortcut to depression.

If depression began on the spiritual path, self-deception can be stated. So we would have to return to the earthly, recognize our borders and learn how to overcome them. Otherwise, you can get stuck in depression until the end of life. And no enlightenment will come.

You pass from passivity to movement. And only from the movement - to high awareness. Until he learns to realize his desires, one cannot immediately pass out from childish fear to awareness.

The way out of depression is the return of desires through awareness of one's fears. When you recognize your boundaries, then you understand where to go next.

It seems that Abraham Maslow said that a person is unhappy if he does not realize his potential.

Imagine that you have the potential, but you are stuck between two chairs: you played enough games for children, and it's scary to tackle adults. Living is boring while taking your comfort zone beyond the borders of the universe. Do not be fooled by this.

When you acknowledge your fears and overcome them, personal strength returns.

Next level: when trained to overcome fear, the level of awareness rises and you notice that there is no future. You are always here and now. Therefore, depression is an illusion. The illusion of a dark future. In mindfulness, it is completely eroded.

Continuous interest awakens to reality when you notice that it looms before you here and now. And you are a co-author of this creation.

The first key to breaking depression is to overcome fears. Learning to feel them. Thanks to this, you establish contact with your desires.

The second key is that you understand that there is no future, it no longer attracts and does not frighten, because you are always in the present. Depression is no longer a place, because it is an illusion of a dark future. In the eternal, interest in living reality remains now.

Confidence and self-doubt

Doubt is a fear of humiliation that gives rise to indecisive and fearful behavior. This is an "echo" of a deep feeling that something is radically wrong with our person, and with our life - like a deep crack that has grown on the body of the soul, like a terrible, ugly flaw that demonstrates its own fundamental defect. That is, it feels as if some initial, incorrigible marriage was laid at the very heart of the soul, and therefore our person is worthless, unnecessary and superfluous in this life. Freedom from this painful experience can be called natural self-confidence.

Self-doubt arises in childhood, when it is not clear why our naive person is honored with love, and for which, on the contrary, indifference and punishment. For what - we do not know, but our unconscious makes its vague conclusion. They love, it means - good, they do not like - bad.

Please note: we do not evaluate our qualities, actions, or even appearance. These contradictory assessments are taken at its own expense by the very core of personal reality - our "I".

The very premise that our gut can be somehow appreciated forms the psychic scale of possible dimensions - from the last insignificance absorbing all the sufferings of the world, to the divine star absorbing worship and adoration.

You can imagine this in the form of a thermometer, where zero division indicates a neutral, natural state, and other links are responsible for illusory deviations in the direction of worse and better.

The "connection" of this psychic mechanism is the main cause of self-doubt. The understanding that one's own "I" can be appreciated, as desired, gives rise to natural anxiety and hypertrophied caution. From here, the whole life drama of a person who is bogged down in endless evidence and excuses of his right to love and respect takes its count. We seize the dazzling chance of a happy endorsement, unaware of its monolithic inseparability with the potential of endless fall.

This built-in mind scale of self-importance is the volume of all possible fixations of self-esteem. And the whole problem is that in general, no one succeeds in strengthening self-esteem at a certain satisfactory level, so as not to settle down below. And as long as the assessment of oneself fluctuates like a limp flag in the wind, there can be no question of any self-confidence.

As a result, we have such a wonderful picture, where each action can threaten a complete and final failure, and small victories inflate the ego to heaven. Claims can be royal, and determination - like a baby. In such dramatic circumstances, where does calm confidence come from?

Compensation of uncertainty

At the top of the psychic scale of our own importance - ideals - all the highest limits of personal realization that our fetishes aim for: love, mania, fanaticism, perfectionism, worship - these are phenomena of the same order. We cling to ideals, believing that we are making a choice of a better life, but in this way we only take root on the psychic scale, the opposite pole of which promises great suffering.

As a rule, gaining self-confidence is of interest only to us, as an opportunity, not looking up from the scale of importance, to approach its highest polarity and feel like a star who has realized her ideal life. That is, we do not strive so much to heal from self-doubt, as we hope to compensate for it with gilded crutches of high conceit.

Imagine a prisoner sitting in a dungeon without doors and guards. He dreams of freedom, of flowering meadows at the foot of snow-capped mountains, but continues to decorate and comfort his dungeon so that the public appreciates his "successes". So we, trying to solve the problem of self-doubt with the help of love and respect of important people, only strengthen the potential of our own humiliation.

Compensating for insecurity with external fetishes is not a mistake, but a necessary measure with which everyone is familiar with experience. For mental health, self-affirmation should not be suppressed, but investigated in practice in order to get fed up with "disease" and get "immunity", and not just another hypocritical grimace.

It is useless to discard a sense of self-importance after reading smart texts. All volitional attempts to become simpler and more confident - nothing more than a continuation of the old game of pride. Previously, the degree on the scale of importance was increased by show-offs, now - by getting rid of them. In this sense, undisguised show-offs are much more honest.

Nevertheless, it is advisable to understand that self-affirmation "cures" not the disease, but its symptoms. Therefore, do not confuse natural self-confidence with pride and conceit. The latter do not relieve insecurity, but only cover it with "beautiful" masks. They all boil down to an external demonstration of their own importance.

Self-doubt is the result of fluctuating self-esteem. Self-affirmation does not solve the problem of uncertainty, but as a drug - it only temporarily reassures "withdrawal," exacerbating the situation by the expanded amplitude of fluctuations in the degree of self-importance. Therefore, the healing process goes along a route where, for a start, self-esteem stabilizes, coming in line with realities, and after that it completely disappears, like an illusory fiction.

At least the relative stabilization of self-esteem is a matter much simpler than the complete liberation of this thermometer of its own importance built into the mind. Therefore, you can start with a simple one - with an honest assessment of real abilities and capabilities. Such realism reduces the degree of uncertainty, because the need to strenuously pose and draw away when the whole truth is already on the face disappears.

For me personally, the complete elimination of self-assessment is, for now, a topic largely theoretical. But there are some glimpses. I know from personal experience and from observations of clients that occupation of the mind with a scale of importance can be at least markedly reduced. That is, feelings about one's inferiority can be reduced at times, up to states where one already has to look for mental stress, and the inside is perceived as simply as the weather outside.

Natural Confidence

Can we really appreciate the epicenter of self - our "I", using the measurements "good" and "bad"? Can we, in general, somehow really evaluate ourselves, without even suspecting who we are? What is our self? How can it be good or bad?

In a sense, we all have an innate self-worth that cannot be measured. That is, our "I" a priori can neither be bad nor good. Both arrogant importance and uncertain flawedness are equally false. Even understanding our worthlessness in the eyes of others does not make our persona worthless and bad "in general".

But as long as the mind is attached to a scale of importance, it perceives the hallucination of its inferiority, like a real sentence imposed by the highest instance of existence. In other words, personal inferiority is not some real fact, but only a strong, irrational faith. We hold on to this illusion because we hope for a stellar win of the highest level on the scale of importance. This topic was covered in an article about a deal with the evil one.

"Bad" is not some real universal reality, but an assessment of the mind - just the thought of something subjectively superfluous. It is impossible to be an objectively bad person. Even the world-famous tyrants receive the most controversial external ratings.

You can be sure that mistakes and miscalculations are definitely "bad". But why on earth? Is spiritual growth possible without experience learned from mistakes and miscalculations? Are mistakes not good in this way?

Self-doubt is treated with awareness and an analytical hunt for private beliefs about yourself and your life. The emphasis is on catching mirages, which are at the heart of the fear of feeling superfluous in this life. To find and neutralize them is not an easy task. Against our conscious will, we bypass our own fears, so even just finding the roots of insecurity is a whole art.

What do I call natural self-confidence? These are any conditions without the shackling fear of humiliation. For example, any actions performed spontaneously without any doubt or hesitation are suitable. Do I need some great confidence to sit on the pot at home? Are we fulfilled by picking our nose? It just happens without any fit to the "right" standards. I intentionally took as an example classes familiar to everyone.

And self-confident people are usually called those who remain calm in situations where excitement and fear are perceived as a general norm. As a rule, these are situations where evaluating viewers participate, in whose eyes our person is afraid to screw up and lose personal ratings. Therefore, so few people can speak in public, take responsibility, knock on closed doors, organize and lead others.

To love the life

I notice that they love their life when they fill it with their favorite content: interesting activities and a pleasant society. So simple. If you do not complicate. But they complicate life and do not understand the banal patterns when they lose contact with their desires. The person does not feel what he wants, loads himself unwanted - and naturally suffers.

Desires are the life energy of the personality, its "food and air". The person finds the visual meaning of life in the fulfillment of desires. And suppressing desires, the person alienates from himself and fades - the most hackneyed path to depression. Follow it with two methods - idealization and fear. I will talk about this further.

Flight and freedom

Desire set two possible directions. They strive either for freedom or for security. These directions usually lead in opposite directions. In the direction of freedom, face to face with fear. In the direction of security, they lose their freedom.

The striving for freedom prompts itself to open and manifest, so that the voice of the soul sounds. In practice, a person simply does what he loves, expresses his uniqueness, risking condemnation.

The pursuit of security forces itself to close and protect, so that the soul is not at risk of being injured. Her voice subsides to a barely audible, and her personality closes, and ceases to feel that in this life she loves — it's too dangerous — to follow the call of her heart. In practice, a person is engaged in anything, just not to risk it. It tries to be inconspicuous by "nobody", merges with the environment so as not to be subjected to possible condemnation.

Only the expression of personal potential allows you to love your life. That is, passing through the barriers of fear is a mandatory challenge on the path of spiritual growth and a joyful life. Suffering is reduced when a person overcomes fears and receives his food - fresh impressions.

Imagine that you have absolutely no fear. What would you do? Allow this fantasy for at least a minute.

You can banally approach a stranger who has attracted attention from the crowd, and at the risk of seeming crazy, still get to know each other. Drive from life is received not in the disgusted four walls, but in unpredictable spontaneity.

Non-existent indestructible barriers

The main trick of striving for safety is such a trick of the mind when one's own fears are taken as ultimate impenetrable walls of existence.

From childhood, everyone feels that the boundaries of the familiar are not the ends of the world, they hide the world of endless possibilities. But if you do not dare to follow them, fear becomes a constant background. So unpleasant that consciousness displaces the experience into the underlying. The understanding of what exactly you are afraid of is lost - but you only feel how the invisible force is grasping the limits of everyday life with a dead grip. And then they confuse their limited, deserted life with global reality. As if everything in general is "perishable and futile being."

In the articles, I have already said that the mind is always drawn to the most comfortable conditions for itself, and from this perspective, each personal stirring is the fulfillment of the current desire. Another thing is that a clear awareness of the desired scenarios of a happy life can disappear altogether when the desire to hide in security prevails.

For example, a person goes to an unloved job, sort of like "forcedly, not of his own free will," but he does it for specific reasons - money, approval, a comfort zone - these "victims" are his current secondary benefit, overpowering the voice of the soul.

Neurotic compulsion is a reluctance to admit that the desire to hide from fear turned out to be stronger than the desire for freedom.

Stereotypes

Another popular way of not loving life by tightly plugging the voice of the soul is the fear of being an abnormal black sheep and the subsequent stereotypical existence. For example, when the soul is dominated by a penchant for creativity, but stereotypes require you to become an office clerk, start a family and get into a mortgage. The example is beaten banal, but reflects popular trends.

Stereotypes with their voracious demands are similar to ideals, but they manipulate not so much a sky-high carrot of success, but a whip of guilt and humiliation for disobeying their dictatorship. You can do justice to stereotypes - they spur on goals that are relatively realistic, in the spirit of: burying a cottage, planting a bonsai, conceive heirs so that they "continue" through them - didn't do it yourself - give way to descendants.

One of my friends, emphasizing his desire for freedom, repeatedly offered his interlocutors a small visualization. If you believe in rebirth, imagine that you built houses and raised children cyclically for hundreds of lives. Presented?

And for the majority, for self-satisfaction all this is really necessary - either nature nevertheless resonates with the standards of society, or it is completely sold to them - and does not know any other comfort. Layers of personality, issued to feed stereotypes, can drown out the voice of the soul to a barely perceptible sadness about something unfulfilled.

Idealization

Another extreme and a way to not love one's life is idealization - its hypostasis: love, fanaticism and deification. In this regard, they fall in love not with people, but with their fantasies about an ideal life. Therefore, the idealization is glorified not only by lovers, but by every prospective harbinger of future happiness, for example, teachers and preachers who advertise those tempting heights with which the mind is selflessly fascinated.

It would seem that everything is wonderful, - here it is a real strong desire - to go along its ideal path and get the desired happiness. And at first the idealist really, as if on the threshold of sparkling success, is overflowing with joy. In contrast to yesterday's life and familiar surroundings, he can feel chosen, awarded a lucky star.

But idealization has a catch that spoils everything quickly. It prompts with all its might to cling to the nonexistent, to accept the dreams divorced from life for impending reality - another false projection. The idealist was initially happy not with real events and people, but with how the present "should" unfold with a future triumph. The idealist has not yet "jumped", but already shouted "gop" at the top of his mouth a thousand times. In your imagination.

A good example is sectarianism, where adherents who believe in fast-paced success are drawn into the abyss of hopes for spiritual laurels. Followers of financial pyramids expect similarly rapid growth, enrollment in the elite, an endless stream of large and easy benefits. And most often they punish themselves with idealization in a relationship when they attribute their only possible happiness to the reciprocity of a lover.

The vagaries of lovers

When a lover confesses reciprocal love, the lover believes that he is handed a ticket to guaranteed happiness, and his hopes flare up with tripled strength. In fact, with his confession, the beloved can express a fleeting impulse of passion, which does not imply any promises. Therefore, a hasty running ahead with the enthusiastic construction of castles in the air of ghostly love guarantees only a departure from reality and the subsequent bitter disappointment.

If disappointment is unbearable, the soul finds a way out in a new reinforced separation from reality, and layers a compacted layer of illusions up to the unconsciousness of madness.

It is not easy for a growing soul to recognize that it has no real power over life and people. There is only an eternal claim to an ideal life. Hanging grievances are a capricious refusal to admit the groundlessness of their requests.

Inflation of love

The main catch of idealization is to discard all past meanings in favor of one decisive one. The idealist "sends to hell" with everything that had pleased him before, as if announcing to the world that he no longer needs it. Alienating himself from all past meanings, he throws all his eggs into one nonexistent basket - that is, nowhere. And when loss is discovered, a gaping hole forms in the soul.

With the beginning of idealization, everything that nourishes the soul, depreciates, interests are erased. And after intoxication with false happiness, a depressive hangover begins. Life in general begins to seem empty and meaningless.

In words, self-deception seems clearly obvious. In fact, everyone fools themselves like that. Such is the nature of the mind - to push aside the real in favor of hopes for the best.

To idealize means not to love your real life, but to put an end to it and despise it, so that it becomes a forgotten step to the feet of a fake deity with transcendental requests.

They are seduced by ideals simply because they like to gamble with hope. And the more fabulous the hope, the more love its plot evokes. Probably, everyone deep down in their hearts feels irrationally special - and therefore worthy of metaphysical mercy.

Falling upwards

On spiritual routes, they also practice escaping to the safety of the comfort zone and fanatical idealization. Escaping from a frightening world is presented as a charitable recluse designed to stifle a person, cutting it off from the desired one so that the consciousness throws it beyond the limits of the personality into the depths of perception.

Careless seekers baptize social paths with mouse fuss and try to break their personality tied to society in order to thus obtain award enlightenment.

Nowadays, the ancient meaning of enlightenment has long been erased, and the concept has become just a fashionable trend to indicate its significance. An adequate person will try on this title unless it is a strategic necessity, realizing how contradictory he is met - with distrust interspersed with blind idealization.

Fanatical seekers receive, as usual, not enlightenment, but lifelong depression, and in advanced cases - a complete separation from reality. A madhouse is not a place, but a state of mind.

A suppressed, devoid of external nourishment person closes on himself, painfully exhausted and fades. Its fragmented remains continue to peer into the desired, and find there a hopeless, frightening emptiness.

Sometimes such self-strangulation really forces one to search for new resources, and the personality begins to draw from itself - first it burns out itself, then goes to the resources of the unconscious. If alienation from oneself has not crossed critical boundaries, the seeker can reassemble himself, crystallize a new layer of personality that resonates with the real.

Therefore, as always, the good thing is that in moderation. A person must receive his "food", his own meanings. Otherwise, immoderately closing on himself, he loses consciousness and falls into despondency.

The state of Buddha is not just an unattainable ideal. Like champion titles in sports. They are reached. Units. But for the average person, faith in their chosenness is almost always idealization - a psychological drug. Even the image of a humble saint can be another "silicone" fetish for the fun of pride. And the contrast with the ideal will poison the soul with guilt and fear of deprivation of the only not impaired meaning.

This is dislike of oneself, rejection of oneself, and attached to them is dislike of life. So-so, and forbidden to be mere mortals.

Recognizing one's own mistakes is the most difficult thing. Otherwise, everyone would have been enlightened long ago. But the psyche knows only one way of healing - and this is the transformation of unrealistic beliefs into the acceptance of the ultimate truth of this single period of time here and now.

How to "dream"?

The main reason for idealization is the inability to separate the possible from the fantastic. The idealist rushes ahead of the "locomotive" of reality merciless to his fantasies.

And so that dreams come true and make you happy, you need such a "trifle" - a sober view of life. If you do not know something for sure, do not believe it. Hesitate. Do not doubt your quality - such torment is fruitless; doubt the "famous." Sincere ignorance leads to the truth.

If you do not feel your potential, do not distinguish between real possibilities, it is not self-doubt that is required, but verification by experience. Successes are achieved by the traveler, every day taking any steps on the way to the desired.

But in order to love life, it's really even more important to switch attention from desired goals to desired processes, which are already pleasing and developing at the same time in the present - this is the recipe for a happy life.

Under the heel and behind the stone wall

No one fully believes in their strengths, in the ability to independently drag their own lives. At heart, everyone feels that he really does not know this life. Therefore, everyone looks at each other in search of answers.

Just as women want to take refuge "behind a stone wall" of male guardianship, so similarly men seek under the heel so that they do not have to think about what to do with their lives.

As a result, the best relationship (for the majority) is just a way not to grow up, not to realize, not to act in order to stay in comfort behind the wing of an older companion, which ideally will provide unlimited support and love.

Sectarians for the same purpose rush to the **feet of the teacher**, where they see protection from the soul-warming illusion of the "right" path.

Everyone wants more confident partners - preferably gods and goddesses - all-knowing, all-perceiving, loving. Therefore, men are looking for a "heel", and women are looking for a "stone wall".

A man is not excited by a self-doubt, weak woman - it seems an infantile daughter. A woman does not respect a weak man - she perceives him with a soft-bodied rag and, again, as a child.

The claimed confidence is not material security and high career levels, but rather - spiritual seniority, the ability to interact with reality boldly and firmly.

Relations for most of us are such a gag from a collision with the unsustainability of life. Relationships plunge into the blissful illusion of security, where one does not have to accept the challenge of the unknown. A partner is needed to serve our involvement in the rainbow mirage of future comfort. The fear of losing this protective mirage saturates the relationship with a full range of negative emotions.

Three types of drama

In psychology, there is one popular theory, on the basis of which, personalities are characterized by three roles: a child, a parent and an adult. Parent indicates, controls and subordinates. The child is naughty and submissive, seeking protection and patronage. The adult does not impose anything on anyone, but takes responsibility for his claims on himself, communicates on an equal footing, and agrees.

Until a person becomes mentally adult, his relationship will turn into a drama, where you can play three roles:

The first option is a heel and a stone wall. The role of a partner-child in a relationship is always a double-edged sword. On one - a sense of security, on the other - everything that is applied to the defense of this feeling: control, jealousy, affection and all the same - a constant alarming background, because they still hide under the heel and behind a stone wall (from fear of real life) .

The second option is to crush with a heel and enclose with a wall. The role of a parent in a relationship is sometimes chosen of their own free will, in order to subjugate, or to bribe with the care of a still beloved partner. But the further he is given to the role of the weak, the less he is perceived as a full-fledged personality - and love is replaced by contemptuous disappointment.

The third option is rivalry. Here, the partners do not feel strength after each other, cannot fully trust, obey - and regularly find out the relationship, as if calling for the second one to become more mature and caring, or to admit that the leader in the relationship is not at all.

Relationships do not turn into drama only for a mentally adult person who does not expect protection from a partner.

Princesses and Princes

With a female claim to the role of material and psychological dependents in society they put up more easily. After all, nature itself endowed the woman with the burdens of bearing and feeding offspring, and the man with the strength to protect his home. But in our time, this ancient given is more often elevated to such an ideal, where a man is a kind of servile servant for the princess, nourished with divine energy.

In words, of course, no man wants a woman's heel. As in the parent-child relationship, you want after all not hedgehogs, but boundless love and care. But children are not only spoiled, but also raised with varying degrees of rigidity. Therefore, under the heel, a yoke of male humility is attached to female patronage.

That is, hoping to remain in a child's relationship under the guardianship of a strong personality, ideally they want to be something like little princes and princesses - such special creatures, created to delight and indulge their whims. But an adult, remaining infantile in the soul, does not cause love and affection among others, but a dismissive pity.

Both men and women remain almost equally at heart in their children, and long for the support and guidance of a superior guide. At progressman.ru, I have already covered this topic in an article about adult children.

How do they become mentally adults?

You can distinguish many paths of spiritual growth, but perhaps the two most obvious are independence and self-sufficiency - that is, the ability to solve your problems and easily endure solitude.

Mental growth is always a difficult way of transforming from a shy position "I don't know and I won't manage myself" to the position "I can not know, but I will manage as I can." That is, it is an acceptance of the challenge of life. A person can recognize his helplessness in front of the unknown, but does not give up and, despite fear, continues to act - solve problems, make mistakes, gain life experience.

A soul-mature personality, as if saturated with itself, easily endures loneliness, therefore it is perceived by others as if a special light shines from its inside. It is sometimes called the inner core.

Such a person is often idealized by projecting on him almost magical features, as if a divine stream flows through his body. And in fact, maybe, just not bad. And that's all.

And if a person suffers alone, he, as if hungry, devoid of his own light, is drawn to the one in whom this light is greater. This is where the legs of affection, jealousy and possessiveness grow.

When a person dares to listen to his desires and actively implement them, the others follow him, because they believe that their leader knows what, in general, is happening and where to move. Leaders replace fathers and mothers.

Heat is generally inherent in relationships — a mixture of warmth and burning drama. Coldness is inherent in solitude - a mixture of bliss with a chilling fear.

There are no right ways. But there are coveted paths where the gut responds with consent. By trusting your life to others, you can find a sense of security, now and then turning into suffocating borders. Trusting yourself, you accept the challenge of the unknown, but you gain a chance for freedom.

Emancipation and sociopathy

In fact, the main process that the psychologist promotes during his psychotherapy is the emancipation of the client. Most mental problems rest on limiting beliefs about how life should be. Therefore, psychologists have to break these beliefs of clients. Separate spiritual and esoteric teachings go further, declaring, in general, all concepts and beliefs false, and liberation from their obsessive influence - for a true spiritual goal, so that becoming enlightened, like a Buddha, a person will be freed from suffering. One slippery milestone lies in the path of this self-liberation - I already mentioned it in the article on the right life, but here I want to say more about this.

All we know is thoughts. Without them, there is neither us nor the world. Everything arises with our "knowledge." Some knowledge is practical and reflect the laws of what is happening. Other knowledge is destructive and leads to empty suffering.

Aiming at perfection, the gut obliges itself to resist the real. As a result, contempt for himself and his life grows because of their inconsistency with invented ideals.

Mental emancipation releases attention previously riveted to the dreams of the mind. A person begins to feel that he is here and now in himself at the epicenter of existence, and ceases to rush life - the race for fantastic ideals stops.

And somewhere here an attentive seeker asks the question: "And what is holding back a person who has no barriers from crime, madness and chaos?"

Emancipation and Sociopathy

You may have heard of a diagnosis such as dissocial personality disorder, or else sociopathy. Simply put, a sociopath is a person whose conscience does not work.

The term is already in fashion, cinema is actively exaggerating it. Images of relatively peaceful, though not the most realistic sociopaths: Dexter, Hannibal, Sherlock, House of Doctor from the same series. They are portrayed by strong and even brilliant personalities. And viewers involuntarily believe that being liberated by a sociopath is even cool.

In the same cinema, almost every killer maniac is exposed as a sociopath. I am not familiar with real statistics, but I admit that the situation is similar. It is logical that a dead conscience removes a number of barriers from the person.

A sociopath is like a predator on a herbivore pasture. He does not feel pity and compassion, and perceives the ideals of good of others as convenient levers for his manipulations.

Sociopathy is formed if a person from an early age receives violence instead of care and love. He wasn't spared in childhood and he isn't trained to spare, therefore he perceives the need for pity for others with cold indifference. Since childhood, a belief has been formed in the consciousness of such a person that one cannot count on love in this world, as if it does not exist at all.

Nevertheless, sociopathy does not imply the inevitable practice of any crime - a person can live and is socially approved.

Here I give an example of this diagnosis to emphasize how ambiguous spiritual liberation can proceed.

The golden mean

Hacking ideals is really fraught with the loss of familiar landmarks. A person ceases to understand why he is forced to be "good" - and this is a double-edged sword. The already crippled psyche really helps the reins of morality to deter fear and guilt from destructive behavior.

It would seem simple - we introduce the rules, suppress the "wrong" - and live in peace. But in the end, it is precisely the inability to express oneself and the gross suppression of the inside that leads to a state where no energy remains to strangle one's own energy; The "valve" breaks down and red-hot emotions are released by an explosive reaction in primitive, impulsive acts, which are condemned by the public formally in the courts and informally by morality.

And if emotions are not completely released, then the psyche becomes enslaved in apathetic alienation, and the body undergoes psychosomatic ailments. So there is no way to become ideal under duress.

On the one hand, beliefs that have grown to ideals provide support - a simplified map of life, where "correct" and "forbidden" directions are indicated. On the other hand, ideals as a whole limit so clumsily that, without any analysis, they suppress not only animal inclinations, but also the natural potential of a person. As a result, the personality itself ceases to flourish, becomes emasculated and becomes an appendage of its own beliefs. This is the same example when the "inner child" is splashed with "dirty water".

I do not at all encourage or justify immoral behavior. But I just say that it is precisely the rejection of self-violence that leads to the natural unwillingness to rape other people as well. Only a free person respects the freedom of others.

A enslaved will be someone else's freedom to envy and be angry, forcing him to be enslaved along with him.

A healthy person does not want to destroy others. We all just want to love ourselves and our life - to accept its real. And forced kindness through gritted teeth for fear of punishment is a mercantile lie that does not contain anything holy in itself.

Freedom

For the untrained psyche, the loss of significant landmarks can result in serious stress, therefore, an intelligent psychologist does not push to total liberation from ideals, but sensitively leads the client through his current lesson. Sometimes new lessons have to be learned on the go, meeting the next stage of emotional freedom together (if the lesson is too complicated, the psychologist should transfer the client to a more experienced specialist).

Therefore, on the site I do not express the most merciless truths to the supports of the personality, but I write cautiously about what the majority is prepared for. The unprepared reader himself denies and closes - and this is in the order of things.

Probably the moral of society, along with the neuroses generated by it, is an inevitable stage of mental growth. But this stage is reevaluated by society. On this site (on the blog and on the forum) we refrain from moralizing, we are talking about freedom and pitfalls on the way to it.

The rhythm of the life

As an illustrative example, there will be physical education classes, but the technique works everywhere - in training, in work, and in everyday affairs.

So interesting is the mind that the same lesson is perceived completely differently depending on the context. For example, when you are unobtrusively invited to an event where you don't particularly aspire, but want to visit rather than not, then the soul remains light - the mind foresees the future horizon as free and varied, as if open to the fulfillment of the traveler's personal desires.

And if you are not invited to the event, but are forced to attend, for example, appealing to duty - in fact, blackmailing with guilt and deprivation of approval, then from this perspective all lightness is eroded, because the event horizon threatens to narrow to a single "obligatory" gauge that does not reckon with personal will of the traveler.

Examples are abstract, and life, of course, is accompanied by an abundance of nuances. Here I wanted to emphasize that the mind does not like compulsion, and when there is a possibility, it resists it with all its might. The mind does not like words like "must" and "should", and always welcomes "can", which implies an open manifestation of personal will.

We can say that a healthy personal will exists only in this format and exists when it comes from honest preference. Otherwise, neurotic willpower remains, poisoned by coercion, when they act not in harmony with themselves, but contrary to their gut.

How to practice useful activities without self-abuse?

You may have noticed that most people who have started sports training abandon classes on average after a couple of months. This does not happen at all because of weak character, but because the planned training is built incorrectly into the usual rhythm of life.

Imagine a mechanism with a conglomerate of programs that it manages. Against the background of thousands of smoothly interacting processes, one small, but quite influential program "Ego Break-through 2017" appears, ordering the system to obey and begin daily intensive exercises. The voice of the program is strong enough to strain the whole system, but it is too presumptuous and incompetent for all existing programs to be rewritten to fit new needs. As a result, the mechanism cracks, glitches, freezes, and in order not to break down completely, it begins to strike.

If you approach the planned tasks and activities realistically, then you wouldn't have to indicate to yourself what and how much to carry out, but first you need to research yourself in order to calculate if there is, in general, the soil for this work, and how fertile it is. And the resistance of the ego is the voice of a small program, naively imagining itself to be the head of the whole psyche.

Self-knowledge helps to calculate your rhythm of life. And do not rush to change it adjusting to new activities; on the contrary, it is advisable to adjust these new classes to your rhythm. Otherwise, the driven inside ceases to listen to the stupid ego, the consent with itself is lost and the internal discord grows.

At progressman.ru, I have already talked about respecting the rhythm of the ongoing life. Similarly, it's useful to sensitively take into account your own rhythm, without being driven into a tight framework.

Imbued with ideas about self-improvement, enthusiasts plan specific activities for self-improvement. And this is all right. Problems begin where plans involve a tight framework. Inspired by the hope for a brighter future, the mind naively outlines concrete planks. For example, decides to go to the gym three times a week for an hour. And if this external plan does not take into account the internal rhythm, then resistance increases with each occupation. As a result, a person who is quite capable of receiving joy from physical education simply throws it away.

In the present, I personally hate to do physical education for an hour or more. Except as an exception. But 20-25 minutes of daily exercises without excessive loads, I have been practicing for many years. There is not even any talk about disruptions, because I do it according to my desire in accordance with the inner rhythm. In the same way, I don't very much like to run for longer than 15 minutes, but I can go for a walk or slowly ride a bicycle in the fresh air regularly for hours.

Adults, like children, really like the movement. We like to jump, run, exercise - the body loves moderate exercise. You just need to catch your rhythm.

There is no need to pull up and push up until exhaustion when the body is already shaking. It is quite possible to maintain and even develop your physical fitness in joy, doing moderate exercises. Let the approach be performed twice as few repetitions of the maximum possible, the main thing is not to exhaust. The body itself will tell you when to take the next step, increasing the load without the threat of breaking out of your rhythm of life.

If the planned activities and activities do not take root and are resisting inwardly, it means that they did not listen to themselves sensitively, and somewhere they ran ahead of the steam locomotive, taking what they wanted to be real - a contrived self-image that was effective for their real rhythm of life.

If the gut protests even against five minutes of classes, then, alas, it will be necessary to admit that the internal alignment in the present does not have any relevance to this topic. Try again in a week, or in a year, when the situation changes.

Of course, there are difficult periods in life when the inside has to put up with long-term ego programs. For example, when students, army, work, parenting. But here you can't deceive yourself in any way. Another student simply needs cheat sheets for a successful five-year term in high school. Employees in organizations stubbornly felony, losing control of uninteresting affairs, or are psychosomatically ill. Spouses sow children to grandmothers, practice irresponsibility, diverge.

And if the mind does not find a way to escape from overload, it goes beyond the mind, or disconnects consciousness from the body.

Therefore, when there is an opportunity, do not rush, do not set the bar too high. Then development will become an unobtrusive game, where the result is no longer as significant as the process.

Right life

Once in childhood, gaining relative consciousness, we find ourselves in this space without coordinates in the chaos of what is happening. And we notice nearby the towering figures of adults. From them we get information about how to live. We take this information on faith, without understanding, because we still do not know how to understand that early age. The world seems incomprehensibly mysterious, almost magical, therefore, in its laws it remains just to believe. All its rules are perceived by default, like sacred rituals of familiarizing with the truth, from which it is "impossible to deviate." Why we can't "never" to the end, we are accustomed to violating this global prohibition (for objectionable behavior) to feel ashamed, guilty - bad and not worthy of the love of god-like, "almighty" adults. We learn to believe what is right, good, and what is false and bad. This is how the deepest motives of emotions are formed - from blind convinced knowledge about what life should be like.

As a result, almost all of our behavior is dictated by a whip of conscience (that is, a fear of humiliation) and a carrot of pride (evidence of our right to love). Hence, the whole maya on the topic of one's own (not) importance and (not) self-confidence.

The psyche is multi-layered. The surface layers are the very ones where we now, with our "adult" mind, begin to "understand everything", and sometimes, we can't do anything. Because in the depths of the soul, children's beliefs have already been sown that have grown to the present abode of the mind in the form of vague feelings. They can already go against the realities for a long time, and at the same time, by virtue of their rootedness, affect the mind and demand their own, much sharper and more persistent, up-to-date, adult views.

As a result, reason and logic with all their productivity, sometimes helplessly capitulate when they absorb children's emotions. No matter how reasonable expediency a person approaches the planning of his "right" life, if these plans contradict his emotions and feelings, counting on their fulfillment will be arrogant naivety.

This is exactly what happens in internal conflicts, where the deep within us grapples with the superficial. At progressman.ru, a recent article on psychoanalysis was devoted to this topic.

These elemental automatic incentives from the past give rise in the present to that very neurotic behavior, taking into account not real situation, but subjective, sometimes openly childish requirements for life.

From here all "must" and "must" come from. It remains for the mind to get out, attributing responsibility for their own irrational claims of abstract morality - they say, "I'm not bliss, but, in general," necessary "and" right. "

Absorption

Absorption in emotions makes a person unstable and chaotic. A man himself does not know what he wants, makes impetuous decisions that he cannot follow. His feelings live their own lives, and, as it were, walk parallel corridors, meeting, perhaps, for internal conflict.

That is, even encountering a frank inconsistency of one's own views, an emotional person is not able to combine his conflicting feelings in order to exhaust the internal conflict. As a result, a person can love and indulge today, hate tomorrow - and so on in a circle with endless cycles.

Relatively speaking, when there are many sagging neuroses in the psyche, they absorb the territory of consciousness. At the same time, the channel of perception narrows, and any intense emotions completely obscure it, loading all thoughts with its energy. As a result, everything that a person is worried about becomes for him the ultimate objective reality - even the most outspoken chimeras are taken at face value. What kind of cinema the mind shows, such a life is perceived without any doubt.

The stronger the emotions capture, the weaker the contact with reality. At the same time, the mind rushes about like a weather vane in the wind, jumps from one plot of a personal fantasy drama to another - in the morning it is happy, in the evening - in horror, it calms down again at night. Experiences depict conflicting roles in personal history: a hero and a loser, victorious and defeated, beloved and despised. Identification with such roles can be all-encompassing, as if the indestructible holy truth is the very one that comes from childhood, strong faith.

Expanded consciousness

When the consciousness remains relatively expanded and the emotions are not absorbed, then the person is able to notice that current experiences are not about life, but about themselves - and they express not their reality, but their own energy. This factor makes it possible to combine and reconcile incompatible desires. They seem to add up to the whole picture, where there is no ground for conflicting motives.

In the process of such reconciliation with oneself, psychic centeredness comes - with it the person understands what he really wants and is capable of stably following without any friction his decisions.

That is, when there are no internal mental conflicts, then there are no internal contradictions, and no special willpower is required to live a productive, healthy life, if that is what you really want.

Conscious, balanced decisions come from a meaningful real "want." Here responsibility is assumed, and not shifted to ideals about how "should" be.

The ability to live and do exactly what you want is a property of a healthy, integrated personality that is no longer torn by internal conflicts. Moreover, a person clearly understands from the depths of his soul that he is not obliged to love, to be good, right, successful, comfortable - he is not obliged, in general, to do anything. His feelings are not a fake grimace to please society, but a real, sincere expression of his nature.

In the end, there is nothing sacred in virtue that is observed solely out of fear of punishment, or the selfish hope of receiving a reward. In this vein, the "righteous" himself is a mercantile liar.

Only a consciously-balanced, responsible attitude to what is happening, without the onslaught of artificial mental debts, leads out of neurosis. Otherwise, all love and kindness become just as artificial and tearful, clutched in the grip of duties.

Very simplistically, the neurotic "knows" how it should be. A healthy person admits that he does not know any reliable coordinates of the right path, but he realizes what she wants in this kaleidoscope of life.

"Blasphemy"

No matter how good and holy ideals are encouraged to be, no matter how beautiful and "right" the way they are drawn, spiritual well-being goes along the route of utmost self-awareness and honesty. All the ideals and beliefs taken on blind faith here, step by step, are investigated and worked out. In a sense, enlightenment - this is such an overthrow of all the sanctuaries imposed.

I understand how ambiguous this statement sounds, as if offering some kind of sacrilege. As a reservation, I want to say that both religious and public morality are not at all evil. In order to maintain order in society, the inspired laws of life remain an urgent need to restrain primitive habits until the individual reaches the stage where he feels the need for a conscious life. And far from everyone needs this.

And a person unprepared for truth can and must practice unconditional faith in a "right" life. And even this text in this case will naturally cause an internal emotional protest.

Then, "betraying" one's own ideals before the established sense does not make sense. Hasty mental relaxation leads to emotional cold and devastation. It is advisable to analyze not everything in a row, but those actual personal "shrines" that specifically today tear the gut into pieces.

Nevertheless, ideals and morality in society are frankly overestimated. Almost everything is moralized, but institutions where they treat the consequences of this plastic surgery of the soul can hardly be found in a medical guide.

However, this does not mean that all religious and public paths are wrong. Life does not fit into these categories. There is just a way - everything that happened is happening and will happen. And "right" and "wrong" are pure, relative conventions.

Say, for cooking dinner, it will be right to use suitable foods. But in everything that concerns life in general and even the specific choice of the next turn on the way, all the rules are sheer convention.

"Right" life

The only criterion for a conditionally "right" life that I personally developed for myself is decisions that you do not regret about the consequences. And regretting nothing is pointless.

And that's all. Next - live as you want. You can rely on ready-made options - why not, you can think with your own head, based on personal preferences.

Truly no one can impose anything on us. Even when we rely on someone else's knowledge and ready-made paths, obey someone's will, this is still our personal choice in the face of the unknown. And responsibility for it should be blamed solely on yourself.

To get out of the captivity of neurosis, there is no other way out than to find that you are constraining yourself to all the boundaries of the "necessary" and the "must" oneself. And it is necessary to discover this not just with a logical understanding, but with an in-depth study of one's experiences.

Behind each emotionally charged conviction of who you are and what you deserve is blind belief. In order to reveal an emotion with all its undercurrents, it is necessary to bite into it - examine thoroughly until exhaustion. Otherwise, these subcutaneous automatisms will become a further fate - the boundaries along which the path will continue.

We never really know what life is and how to live "right." There are no real coordinates for the correct path. There is only this, already happening, uncouth, sometimes ordered, sometimes wild reality. Whatever dreams position hopes, all of them somehow devastatingly lose to what is already there - this silent inevitability called "life".

Fidelity, betrayal and free relationships

Fidelity in society is idealized, and without any critical analysis is accepted as an undoubted value. Treason, on the contrary, is demonized - it is perceived as a sinful evil. As psychological practice shows, most of all the problems in our heads arise precisely on the basis of beliefs that are taken for obvious truths. Sometimes, before swallowing a dish, it is advisable to familiarize yourself with its ingredients. Today we will analyze the "recipe" of betrayal and fidelity. If the topic is not relevant for you personally, you can consider the article as a good example of a critical analysis of "divine" false truths.

I do not call for infidelity and free sex here. In the article, on the contrary, real grounds are considered for fidelity, to believe in it, as if in a Christmas miracle, was not necessary.

In our society, it seems clear to everyone that betrayal is "bad" and loyalty is "good." In psychology, such blind moralization is seen as a mechanism of psychological defense - the way in which personal claims are covered by "certain" values. That is, it's simply convenient for us that the partner believes in his obligations, as in the holy laws of life, without exposing them to "sinful" doubts.

When it is scary to lose your happiness, to feel cheated, unnecessary and abandoned, when it is clear that there is nothing to keep a partner in the relationship, then it is beneficial to believe in the duty of fidelity precisely blindly, as in an undoubted, divine law. We hold on to our values because they justify and cover our neurotic fears.

If we depart from blind moralization, the picture no longer seems so unambiguous. Treason cannot be something absolutely "bad", but fidelity is "good". It all depends on the conditions and views.

Conditions and views

It could be greatly simplified and said that cheating is "bad" simply because it hurts. But this logic is inconsistent, medical procedures are also painful, and they do not become "bad" from this. Moreover, only the injured party is hurt here; the cheater, on the contrary, receives the joy of "forbidden" pleasures.

It could be said that treason is "bad" because it destroys relations. But with the same success, betrayal becomes a blessing, because it eliminates the initially not reliable partnership.

For example, we can take a more complicated situation, where relations do not end with treason, but continue, poisoned by guilt, resentment and jealousy. But here, it is impossible to say that violated fidelity is something unambiguously "bad". After all, relationships are maintained, and betrayal just pulls the truth to the surface - the real attitude of the partner who changed, fear and dependence of the injured party. And it's useless to be offended by the truth. It remains only to recognize the naivety of one's own expectations and draw constructive conclusions.

But what about fidelity? Is she so good? There are many examples to the contrary. When, for example, a person is financially and psychologically independent, of course, in order to preserve his infantile qualities, loyalty to a partner is extremely necessary. Treason in this position becomes a healing kick from the swamp of the comfort zone.

Another example is when people, being incompatible, somehow miraculously converge, and in order to disperse, they lack decisiveness; and in this case, fidelity in vain preserves unpromising and worthless relationships.

The most common fraud that fidelity supports has recently been parsed on progressman.ru in an article on ownership. There is no reality where a partner becomes our property. And if betrayal destroys this greedy illusion, then stands on the side of truth. Relationships are not a duty or a given, but an opportunity that partners are free to use based on personal discretion.

Another case of fidelity is blind observance of moral or spiritual virtue. Treason in this vein is regarded as a sin, from which the cheater is somehow made a "bad" person. But just think, what is good and holy in virtue, which is observed solely out of fear of punishment, or the selfish hope of receiving a reward? Is not the "righteous man" himself a mercantile liar in this case? As I see it, there is no righteous fidelity. But there is a simple, sincere and natural desire to maintain and maintain the relationships you value.

In all the above examples, treason is not some kind of tragedy, but something like a cold, sobering soul, after which it becomes more and more difficult to continue the practice of self-deception. Sometimes a lie is so sweet that reality, metaphorically speaking, has nothing left to do except to directly poke a person with his nose into his own self-deception.

Why, in general, keep fidelity?

To begin with, I'll give a couple of not very constructive examples.

Nobody likes to feel cheated, unloved and unnecessary. And we all know how to do this. We can say that fidelity for the most part is a bit of an unspoken social contract for not causing this neurotic pain to each other.

And it's wonderful when the partners manage to agree and trust each other. But if the fear of being deceived occurs without any reason and makes you torture your partner with empty jealousy and extortion of evidence of great and pure love, then you should be able to recognize the existence of a personal problem, which for good should be solved not at the expense of the partner, but with him in constructive cooperation, or already independently. If the result does not work out, the psychologist will help you.

Another reason to abstain from treason is the aforementioned virtues. Even the most rational and sober-minded people deep down are very afraid of being "bad" and "wrong," and therefore not worthy of love and approval. Often this fear is reinforced by an unclear, but firm belief in the existence of higher powers that tirelessly spy on us in order to identify possible reasons for revenge for our "wrong" actions. Loyalty in this vein is practiced as a necessary measure of salvation from mystical punishment.

A bit about the "punishment".

At a practical level, treason is punished in a simple and obvious way - traitors are condemned, deprived of trust, and their lightweight approach does not allow creating reliable, trusting relationships with deep mutual understanding. This is how "mystical punishment" acts on the side of the traitor.

On the "victim" side, treason is usually perceived as a vile betrayal, as if a traitor was blissing out at the expense of his partner's suffering. In fact, the injured party punishes himself in the same way with his uneven perception of the situation. The propensity for jealousy, a sense of ownership, attachment, unrealistic expectations - all this is real karma, which spontaneously leads to obvious, logical consequences without any mysticism.

That is, betrayal as a treacherous "evil" is not an act, but an attitude to the situation. For some, it's a complete punishment, tragicomedy and drama, for others, a calm statement of facts - they say, "Well, yes, the relationship ended because the partner was carried away by someone else. It happens to everyone? We will continue to live. ”

Feeding neurosis and moral ideals are not the only reasons for maintaining marital fidelity. Healthy fidelity is well expressed in relationships of reliable business partners. They can trust each other and strengthen partnership for the common good.

Take, for example, such a joint “project” as procreation. A woman's male fidelity during pregnancy and breastfeeding is necessary as a guarantee of support in this unprotected position. A man, if he wants his family with a child, to spoil relations with his mother is also unreasonable. After all, she not only brings up and feeds the child, but with high probability becomes for him the closest person and inevitably affects his views - including the opinion of his father.

Another reason for healthy fidelity, no matter how simple it may sound, is trust and intimacy. This is a feeling when the soul is light only from the fact that somewhere nearby there is this close and dear person. You can just be silent and go about your business - and this warm, expanding the boundaries of the mind light will hold on. From personal experience I can say that such an experience has nothing to do with dependent attachment.

Another interesting reason for fidelity is in-depth self-knowledge through emotional connection with a partner. Two can not only exchange experiences, but as they are ready to study personal depths through the systematic disclosure to each other of the most intimate, “unlike” territories of their own souls.

Earlier, I talked about the "benefits" of betrayal, which destroys the illusion of owning a loved one. Here, in fact, not everything is so simple. In the same article about the feeling of ownership, I also said that possession with a big caveat can nevertheless be considered something real just in the case when partners manage to maintain reliable, strong relations for a long time. Under such conditions, banal statistics are on their side. Relations lasting for many years are very likely to continue the next day.

As mutual trust develops in reliable relations, the beneficial aspects of relations as such can grow: emotional and material mutual assistance, knowledge sharing, the ability to act in concert with a double force, convenient separation of duties and delimitation of areas of control, consideration and resolution of problems from different reference points, and much, much more. In general, similar partnership principles work in all areas.

Free relations

Free relations are practiced so as not to be burdened with obligations. Free relations save not only obligations, responsibilities, rights, they, if you look, free partners from each other in general. In such a weak and unstable relationship, it is almost impossible to feel and predict mutual support, and loneliness can become a constant companion.

In a free relationship, partners are essentially distanced lovers who practice a variety of sex without cause for deep intimacy. And this is quite a healthy approach.

Sometimes professing free relations is attributed to maturity and independence, because they seem to be "free" from jealousy and affection. In fact, in such a "mature" relationship there can be anyone, sometimes just out of hopelessness, because the beloved does not want anything "serious", and occasionally is quite happy to meet without any obligations.

Introverts are more inclined towards stable relationships - it is too troublesome to search for new partners each time. Extroverts in free relationships can chase changes and new experiences. Regardless of temperament, such a style of relationship may be the only alternative to contact with the opposite sex due to inability to get along with someone on a serious basis, or in such rare cases when loneliness really pleases.

Free relations are constantly exposed to the threat of complete termination, there is no certainty in them, and the partner, checking himself in proximity with others, at any moment may feel that "there" on the side is more interesting to him.

Sometimes the seekers of impressions hang in such "freedom" for a long time, because they are carried away by the novelty of the first intimacy, or they hope, having sorted out the maximum of partners, to choose the "ideal". Something logical is present in this idea, but in fact any new relationship is such a "short film" with a plot that no one knows beforehand. Everything can end quickly and sadly, can turn into a long drama, or really - into something beautiful.

Free relations in themselves are not something bad, but there is one spiritual threat in them, which not everyone is ready to face. As I see it, relationships without obligations in the consciousness of an individual devalue the ideal of love without offering anything in return. As a result, a gloomy, meaningless emptiness remains in the soul, in the place of which there was once a hope for finding happiness in close proximity with a partner. Sex in free relationships can give off a tinge of dirt just because it breaks the ideals of love and fidelity.

It would seem, why, in general, for partners to shackle each other with some kind of artificial framework and obligations? After all, if they want to be together and to know each other, they do not need to sign any agreements and hang on to each other the right of ownership. Everything is sincere and natural. But the fact is that we after all cannot surely know about the seriousness of the partner's intentions - whether he wants to build a house with us, or just went for a walk. Sounding your own mood for something serious and reliable can spur a similar mood in a natural way and in the mind of the partner. It seems like, "let's carry out this large-scale project together?" Returning to the analogy of business partners, obligations are necessary so that the "project" of relations does not develop randomly, but in a constructive manner.

Conclusions

A difficult thing - relationships - tricky. Everything seems to be clear, but if you dig it up - a bunch of questions and doubts - an illusion on an illusion. They expect love, harmony and happiness, but they get burning drama and lifelong trials. But they continue to believe and hope that the whole thing is in the "right person" - you just need to "re-educate your partner, or find" that same "one and then there will be" happiness ".

This approach is only partially true. Of course, as in friendship, not everyone can have a relationship with us. But a suitable partner is only part of the success. Roughly - about thirty percent. The remaining interest depends on our person. Whatever partner is next to us, relationships with him reflect our own persona with all her real qualities. And if the mind is seething with fear and general dissatisfaction with life, all this will inevitably color the relationship.

Therefore, it makes little sense to idealize fidelity and condemn treason. As long as we don't know ourselves, we don't understand what we want, and we don't really realize what we are worried about, instability in relations is a natural consequence that cannot be avoided. And no artificial guidelines will help the cause. The best thing you can do is to stop chasing beautiful ideals and honestly accept that we are still learning relationships, literally on the go in "combat" conditions, and therefore mistakes and miscalculations are not some personal collapse, but practical experience necessary for spiritual growth

.

Emotions are a real source of problems

At some stage I tell almost all clients how problems arise. I say that it's all about emotions. In life, events happen - that's how it works. And those of them that are painted with unpleasant emotions are what we call problems. That is, as a result, it is this mental pain that has to be treated. Then both the attitude and the approach to events change - without negative feelings, they cease to seem like problems.

Emotions are usually described tautologically as an evaluative, biased attitude. Here I express my unscientific look again. The article turned out to be difficult for me in the sense that it took a lot of time to reflect my own observations in more or less accurate formulations. He deleted and rewritten some paragraphs even once, until the topic sounded at least relatively close to how I see it. And still the theoretical model is still damp. Have the courage to doubt everything below.

Subcutaneous automatisms

If you look closely at how we make a choice, how, in general, we act, then on the surface of consciousness these personality-controlling levers feel like our own impulses. However, in some impulses we do not hesitate to acknowledge our real desires, while others seem alien, as if something from the inside, bypassing our will, are forcing us to our elemental goals, divorced from the conscious personality program.

When I thought about these underlying motivators, the phrase "subcutaneous automatisms" spontaneously came to mind. These are long-standing desires that began to live their own lives. We can forget about what we once wanted, but desire has already unfolded on the territory of the psyche, appropriated a part of our life energy and developed into emotion.

Today's situations can remind our unconscious of the past, where there were unfulfilled emotions. In the present, they awaken and shoot unexpectedly, like hell out of a snuffbox, demanding implementation.

That is, once these requirements were conscious and felt as their own. But later, not being realized, for the time being they hid. Over the years, a person grows, changing attitudes, approaches. But subcutaneous automatisms are planted so deeply in the soul that the current personality transformations may not affect them at all - just some insignificant ripples somewhere far on the surface of the "ocean" of the psyche. Therefore, floating up in the current situation to that very "surface", ancient emotions, at times, seem elemental and alien, as if a person had become obsessed with some otherworldly force.

An aggressive variety of deep unconscious impulses is superstitiously called internal demons. And this is nothing more than our own desires, for which we refuse to bear responsibility.

These individuals of fermentation, separated from the general canvas, until we recognize them, in a sense, really live their own lives. They can appear in dreams, expressed in "strange" situations and unusual actions of the person.

Most of the emotions are dictated by such offscreen levers. Therefore, it is so difficult to control emotions - they arise as if by themselves, like a flood. As a result, emotions control us simply because they arise from such bowels of the soul to which the daily consciousness has no longer been allowed.

Emotion coordinates

For reference:

Emotions are often confused with feelings. Usually feelings are described as a kind of established emotional attitude, for example: stable love or hatred of a person. Emotions, as opposed to feelings, are situational and short-lived - a kind of sensual impulses.

The term "feelings" is ambiguous; it is also used for bodily sensations when talking about the five senses. Therefore, in the article, in order to avoid confusion, I use only the term "emotions" in general terms. In addition, as I see it, feelings are such "abnormally" protracted emotions. I will talk about the reasons for this delay.

Emotion is the energy of intent, designed to charge specific actions. Most emotions have two reference coordinates along which they move - this is "target" and "defeat".

The intention of emotion is the determination to fulfill a goal. With the advent of intention, emotion flares up and motivates, pushes toward the goal and repels from defeat. Externally passive emotions, such as sadness, resentment, or self-pity, possess these properties.

The goal is "victory", the achievement of a condition under which the intention of the emotion is satisfied, and the emotion ceases to be produced, releasing the energy that it occupied in order to "sound".

Defeat is a forbidden condition under which the goal of an emotion is recognized as completely failed. In this case, emotion, again, ceases to be produced.

Disappointment is another condition (the most common) under which emotion dissolves. This is a situation where the goal of an emotion is recognized as irrelevant, no longer of value. Most often, frustration happens when an emotion reaches its goal.

Partial disappointment can be distinguished - this is when the value of the goal of emotion decreases, and the strength of the emotion decreases.

Emotions are initially neutral energy, filtered and colored by intentions. The taste of a separate emotion, as it were, recalls this specific intention, leads along the route of its implementation. This taste is always twofold - the anticipation of success and the fear of failure are mixed in it. The more significant the intention is perceived for life, the more energy is released under it, the more powerful is the emotion.

Lingering emotions

The emotional problem (mental suffering) is not even in the failed intention of the emotion, but in the approach to failure. It is the deviation from the goal (or at least its anticipation), and the movement towards failure that causes suffering - a situation that is usually called the problem.

Depending on the proximity to the goal, emotion changes taste. The approach is encouraging in anticipation of victory. Deviation from the goal threatens a forbidden failure, and colors the emotion with an aura of hopelessness.

The main problem of emotions is that they often never reach any of the end points - neither goal nor failure. And therefore, they sag at idle between these poles, either encouraging us with victory, or plunging us into despair, an approaching defeat.

Such unfinished emotions tend to accumulate and accumulate in the unconscious layers of the psyche. There, in the depths of our souls, intentions of emotions literally parasitize on our vital energy. They, like insatiable drones, constantly consume it. And in return they give vague dualistic experiences ("taste" of emotions).

Suppressed emotions are an eternal loss. An ordinary adult man carries a whole cascade of such unresolved problems, already not really understanding what makes his soul so sick and what makes him happy. Each stir of reality touches some internal strings - one or several of these internal polarities at once - our emotions.

The internal split

Emotion is energy, they charge and give strength. And everything would be alright if this energy were always directed to something constructive and certain. But we with our superficial mind very often notice how out-of-place emotions work, and we simply crush them, not even suspecting what catastrophic consequences this is fraught.

Thus begins the internal schism, where the superficial mind conflicts with deep feelings. And it turns out such a wonderful situation, where a person, seemingly with all his soul interested in his own well-being, is fighting against himself and the world is losing in his soul.

Metaphorically speaking, inside us the internal child and adult compete for the right to control. The child has the main reserve of vitality and childhood desires. An adult has a relatively mature mind and a pointer with which he tells the child what is possible and what is not.

At the same time, unsatisfied deep desires not only continue to look for a way out, but along the way bring a sense of threat that they will not be able to be satisfied (the approach of "failure"). And our deep children's mind perceives this threat as mortal, and it shakes in earnest.

As a result, an adult already states that his life seems normal according to external criteria, and maybe successful, but it's hard on his soul, and sometimes it's scary to hell. His inner child is desperate and sheds tears.

Eternal bummer

Life energy is expended frankly absurdly. Inwardly, she directs her to her desires, and the superficial censor presses this energy embodied in emotions, leaving her without a decision.

As a result, there are no strengths, and the soul hurts, and it's a shame for emotions - there's not enough to crush them, so you also have to repent for the fact that they generally arise (and this is another emotional vicious circle). Indeed, it is "supposed" to be smart and collected, and not impulsive emotional.

The unsatisfied intentions of suppressed emotions continue to be fueled by energy, as if in the hope that they will nevertheless be satisfied. That is, internally, over and over again, ascertains an unresolved problem and endlessly challenges fresh solutions of energy - our emotions - to solve it. And the superficial mind simply displaces them into the unconscious. "Until better times".

And so in a circle. A mechanism honed over the years. As a result, the crushed problems do not go anywhere, but sag an eternal painful background.

Thus, even in depression, a person always has energy. It's just that she is crushed somewhere deep inside - this offscreen psychic dynamo was saddled by his repressed desires. And on the surface there is no desire or strength left.

Suppressed emotions become the reason for the eternal breakdown - the familiar feeling that here and now there is always something missing, but just to live and enjoy is not a dream come true.

Eternal childhood

Even "passive", children's emotions, outwardly expressed by resentful crying, are still an active, fulfilling intention. A child cannot yet achieve his goals in other ways.

For example, in childhood, we seem to understand without any words that the universe is about our problems. As soon as you regret yourself, wept bitterly, as help immediately comes. And if the maneuver does not work, then you need to feel sorry for yourself three times stronger and not just cry, but sob in three streams.

As we grow older we can discover the stupid unproductiveness of self-pity. But something inside, bypassing all rationality, can, according to an ancient habit, induce this practice. And this something acts infinitely convincingly, with firm knowledge insisting on its own. So, it seems, an adult, sane person with a half-turn becomes a capricious child, and in bitter cry expects some kind of obscure pity support.

The problem of children's emotions is that they are initially passive and do not work in everyday life that requires active actions. Meanwhile, they are spending no less energy than apparently active intentions. But the conviction of the legitimacy of one's own claims under the charge of infantile feelings can be so powerful that even an adult can easily conduct them. And offended as sincerely as once in childhood.

Self-justification

Here on progressman.ru I often talk about how arbitrary "good" and "bad", "obligatory" "correct" and correctable "wrong" are, how uncritically we swallow them, taking them at face value. All these semantic connectives - about emotions - our irrational addictions. How blindly we crush them, just as blindly we follow their influence.

No matter how inappropriate and wild the emotion may seem, the mind will do everything to justify it, will tie to the rationale all possible rationalizations - even the most ridiculous ones. While the emotion sounds, filtering yourself for adequacy is extremely difficult. The emotions are acted upon without understanding, without understanding their own intentions and possible consequences, as if unconditionally trusting that blind conviction with which the emotion is charged.

The less clarity there is in the consciousness, the weaker the "face control" crawling out of unconscious motives. In this situation, the most destructive actions will easily seem justified and legitimate.

In any business, personal addiction tends to distort the overall picture of what is happening with excuses of personal gain. So we are arranged. Without looking back, we act on the emotions, sometimes, not even close noticing how we behave by the nose.

Consciousness

So it turns out that the suppression of emotions, and free expression can be equally stupid. One leads to psychosomatic ailments, the second leads to destructive eventual consequences.

And in any case, the roots of feelings can persist, leading to relapse. That is, other emotions can be satisfied forever, so completely and not satisfied, and the unconscious will again and again slip the same bitter candy in new wrappers.

Finally and without any kickbacks, the problem is solved when the initial motive of emotion (which is at the origins of this problem) is realized with full clarity.

That is, when we understand what exactly we really wanted, then it turns out without any suppression of desires to really outwit. Literally immediately lets go.

An experienced psychologist periodically finds these special moments when his client, finally having regained responsibility for his own deepest desires, finds relief. Energy ceases to be spent on unproductive emotion, and when released, it returns part of personal strength.

The process of such awareness is not an easy task. Emotions are such charged unconscious understandings - often vague, blurry and global. Therefore, they are not easy to specify and neutralize. There are many techniques. At the same time - not a single freebie. Everywhere you have to work, and to study yourself tightly.

Sometimes careful observation of one's own experience is enough to unfold it and bring the original intention from the unconscious to the "scene" of direct awareness. Sequential analysis sometimes works more productively, where common sense is complemented by an intuitive observation of the situation as a whole.

In this case, you do not need to persuade yourself and convince yourself of responsibility for emotions. The mind is already inclined to intellectualize and rationalize, in order to at least explain and appropriate its "unauthorized" emotions to itself at least with some nonsense. Own original motives must be precisely realized, and not convinced of their authorship.

This article is just a brief look at the subject. In practice, there are always hundreds of nuances that do not fit into the framework of the article. I will continue the topic.

I wanted to write a couple of paragraphs about how little and shallow science has studied emotions, no one really says that they know what it really is. But I quickly realized that I was digging the topic unreasonably. Nevertheless, the definitions that I met in psychological literature really look superficial, and reveal not the essence of emotions, but rather their external manifestations.

In addition to emotions and feelings, moods are of no small importance in life - they are finer and longer than impulsive emotions, live like the taste of the surrounding space, and set the atmosphere for the ongoing life. I'll probably write about them separately.

Resentment is called upon to blame in order to receive a "just" retribution. Anger is aimed at the rapid defense of personal boundaries. Excitement is looking forward to victory. Pity encourages saving. Perhaps interest is one of the few emotional experiences that does not imply mandatory goals, but feeds the process (of learning).

***

There may be a fair doubt, where can the baby come from? But he does not understand anything, because there is no personality there either. And yet, what we call emotions, in general, implies at least a vague anticipation of a possible goal. I can't know this, but much indicates that in some primordium, goal-setting is even characteristic of animals.

***

Imagine a tyrant ruler with a split personality disorder. He built a factory in the city, draining the main city resources. He arranged half of the townspeople there, who under a mortal threat gave a categorical decree - to produce the so-called "final goal of intent" - and promised for him his eternal supportive love. At the same time, the second half of the city ultimately ordered, under the threat of public shame, to interfere with this ultimate goal - and for success promised honor and glory.

As a result, one part of the city is shaking from the fear of death, hoping for the favor of the ruler, the second - from fear of possible shame and in the hope of eternal glory. And both with each other - in a collision. Not being able to achieve their goals, they periodically find themselves at the threshold of final failure.

The remaining grains of residents who were not involved in this civil war are only quietly surprised at how stupidly the city is spending its resources - on the uninterrupted maintenance of the conflict in throwing between hope and fear.

Familiar situation?

***

Talking about our life, we tend to talk about events, missing the fact that what is happening to us has absolutely no meaning without the "taste" that emotions and feelings create. Without emotional fullness, all our thoughts are only dry, faded "containers". Even the most pragmatic and callous people are guided by the very same sweet carrots of emotions and feelings that this pragmatism gives rise to in them.

Decision-making

It is decision-making that determines real life. Everyone at another time asks himself: what choice to make? Is the decision correct? Are we not fooling ourselves? Decisions can be influenced by the voice of conscience, the opinion of authorities, moral principles, laws of the state, and religious virtues. As a result, a person is torn under the dictates of many influences and no longer understands what he really wants.

First of all, I want to say that decision making makes us mentally adult. The child does not know life and trusts parents - all responsibility for them. Making a really serious decision is scary for a child, because taking responsibility for one's life means growing up - deprivation of support and becoming on one's path. Such a deprivation of support is fraught with a fear of the unknown - a sensation as if behind the next turn could be anything. Therefore, most people do this all their lives and remain adult children, who find it easier to shift responsibility for their lives to elders, to the state, or to circumstances. Independent decision making and responsibility for personal choice is a spiritual growth.

I believe that everyone can and should live as he wants, and here, no matter how naive or pathetic it may sound, it is worth trying to listen to your own heart. Otherwise, the decisions taken will inevitably be colored by doubts, and lead to dubious results, respectively. However, self-deception is sometimes so subtle that to understand what you really want is simply impossible. It is then that mistakes are made, and the choice leads to disappointment.

Among spiritual seekers it is fashionable to consider mistakes and problems as necessary lessons, without which there is nothing to learn. With this look, I completely agree. Overcoming difficulties, we develop the power of distinguishing a new order, and begin to make decisions more consciously.

And yet, our self-deception knows no limits. The ego is constantly thinning out, inventing increasingly tricky ways to fool itself. In deep meditation, it becomes clear what all our concepts of life are - a homogeneous mass of energy without beginning and end, without support and essence, and without final meaning. However, maintaining such an understanding in society is extremely difficult, and sometimes even completely impractical. Decision making takes place the more efficiently, the more realistic we evaluate our goals and opportunities.

Realism is important not so much in a sober assessment of external phenomena, but in sobriety manifested in relation to oneself. The less confusion there is in the head, and the more clarity there is, the more distinct the voice of intuition can sound. It is impossible to come to the truth, building a path out of self-deception.

Sometimes, I don't feel like weighing or analyzing anything. A person knows what he wants here and now, and then - be what happens. However, decision making based on superficial desires leads to superficial results. The pursuit of pleasures in order to continuously satisfy desires as soon as possible leads to the depletion of all external and internal resources. Wisdom is foresight. It is important to be able to rejoice in today's efforts, understanding that in the future they can pay off.

In the end, if neither conscience nor logic with intuition is heard, but nevertheless, I want to make a more or less balanced decision, it is quite appropriate to rely on religious and moral postulates - they exist to influence decision making when no confidence in one's own free will.

If you believe the Eastern teachings, according to our karma everything that happens to us that we ourselves have created happens to us - we accept the fruits of our own decisions. Everything that happens is the result of our own activities. Everything that a person once gave away to reality also comes back to him, sometimes to an increased degree. You can take into account the laws of karma just in case. But in general, the fact that each action has its consequences is an obvious fact, and these consequences are multifaceted. This topic on progressman.ru devoted article on sins and morality. Decisions made affect our relationship with both the outside world and the inside. Conscience can both reward and punish.

It is important to remember that not everything that is good for us will be good for others. Decision making can have a diametrically opposite effect depending on the conditions. The laws of karma are not some kind of revenge of fate. The consequences of our actions are "returned" to us - that's all. Life simply demonstrates clearly what those factors led to - states, feelings and thoughts that influenced the decisions made. Karma is our experience.

If life, war, conflict, disease dominate, it is possible that in this way conscience at an unconscious level eradicates from the soul violence and inattention to the living. When we understand what pain is, then we feel that reality deserves respect and decision-making, then, as if by magic, it turns to our person the same side.

Some careless seekers sometimes add to the ideas of complete "looseness", "detachment" and "controlled" stupidity, which often result in buffoonery, cunning, arrogance, disrespect for others, a convenient excuse for lust, irritation, deception, etc. All these experiences are ultimately as a result, they turn against the one who performs actions under their influence. From the very beginning it makes sense to be honest with yourself, and clearly understand the motives that influence decision making. And if, for example, anger arises, any excuses at the event level are self-deception. It is necessary to recall the key factor that all reality is a projection of our mind. Events are colored by our karma, they do not create experiences, they only "release" them.

Some spiritual teachers do use unusual methods, play, and unnatural behaviors during training, in order to teach them in this way in accordance with the student's qualities. Especially vividly are such methods expressed in Japanese schools of Zen Buddhism, where monks are led to the truth in a direct way outside of concepts.

Decision making at this level is intuitive, and in each case deeply individual. An enlightened master, in order to save the student from mental constructions, and convey to him how far the words are from the truth, can use bizarre gestures, arrange "senseless" and dangerous situations, in such a way causing the student's mind to shut up, stop so that he sees reality as it is - out of concepts. One famous master, when asked about the nature of the mind, broke a jug, which symbolically demonstrated the illusory nature of the barrier between the external and the internal.

The unusual behavior typical of Zen masters, pressure and cunning without any bad karmic consequences, can probably only be afforded by a real enlightened person who precisely feels what a student needs in the current situation in order to advance on the path.

Making decisions is a kind of response to life. And the more refined the perception we have, the more accurate, and sometimes inexplicable to the mind, this response becomes. In other situations, inappropriate behavior is a banal show off.

A Zen master can give his student a koan, an unsolvable riddle, or a question that the student can sometimes meditate for several years. One of the most popular koans: "what does the sound of one palm sound like?" In general, almost every koan can be reduced to the question of how what happens cannot happen. If the student is a beginner, he might think that the riddle has a logical solution, and then, having arrived at the master with the answer, he gets a slap in the face. The answer to such a riddle is, first of all, the state of the student, and not his words. Decision making at the level of the mind is limited, therefore, for example, in emergency situations we act spontaneously, doing the impossible.

There are no insoluble questions. Each question contains the root of the answer. A koan is a mystery beyond logic and meaning - a riddle, the answer to which lies in an intuitive, illuminating layer of consciousness. In order to survive the "answer" to this riddle, a one-pointed mind, by meditating on a paradoxical question, raises consciousness into the realm of reality where everything is possible, where there are correct answers to any insoluble contradictions, where everything exists and does not exist at the same time. Making decisions on an intuitive level is exactly the same as finding an answer to the riddle of a koan. There is no doubt at this level of consciousness, and the right decisions come spontaneously.

Problem solving

Conscious choice

Whatever the problem, for starters it's enough to honestly ask myself: "what am I worried about? Can I do something about this problem? " We worry when we feel that we are not doing enough to solve our problems, not everything we are capable of, or we are evading them at all, but we refuse to acknowledge our indecision and irresponsibility. As a result, the mind sags in a painful suspension, and instead of taking immediate actions to improve its situation, practices passive nagging.

The baby has no choice but to burst into tears louder, drawing attention to his misfortune to solve his problems. But over the years, this childish manipulation is becoming less and less productive, and already causes nothing but empty suffering. And it seems that adults seem to be practicing it, just according to a long-standing habit, while it seems to them that simply worrying about the injustices of life is easier than accepting their own weakness and real unwillingness to solve their problems.

A psychologically adult person, when she really does not want to solve a particular problem, just realizes this and consciously accepts this choice - to remain passive and inactive. The more conscious and firmer the choice, the less doubt and soil for experience.

Conscious choice is the way out of a painful state of suspense. Until this choice is made, an anxious feeling remains, as if something is being missed. At progressman.ru, a separate article is devoted to the topic of conscious choice.

No one can, otherwise

you only do what you can. If you can get up and start doing something, then get up and do it. If you can't, there isn't enough motivation, and it's easier for you to sit silently and passively, doing nothing, even if this choice is firm and conscious. Only having determined your choice, you stop indulging, tormented and sorry.

And there's nothing to regret. "No one can do otherwise," I think I read this wise phrase for the first time somewhere from Gurdjieff. And I was hooked. I pondered this phrase, and trying on my life, made it an installation that put a lot in its place. It is completely pointless to regret what was done or lost. In the past, you were exactly the kind of person who could lead this life just as he had already spent it. It simply could not be otherwise. If it were otherwise, it would not be you, but some other person with a different life.

In fact, our whole life choice develops in two directions: we either act and actively solve problems, or inaction while remaining passive. In such inaction, we either calm down and humbly accept the circumstances, or commit stupidity and begin completely senseless torment about our "unfortunate" fate. Carlos Castaneda called such torment indulgence.

Indulgence

In the Catholic Church, indulgence refers to evidence of absolution. To indulge is to forgive sins for oneself, to indulge one's weaknesses, to regret and justify oneself, swelling up to the limit in these experiences. Indulging is the best way to not solve your problems, bring life to the uttermost desolation, and become a crying loser who has no choice but to complain about the injustice of life.

Indulging compensates for their own passivity. There is a choice: either to deal with problems and directly establish a life situation, or instead of these reforms to engage in self-flagellation. Why act and solve problems if instead you can just worry about it? Why correct mistakes if instead you can just torture yourself with guilt? Why change something if you can feel sorry for yourself instead? Why so many extra gestures, if you can sit still, suffer softly, blaspheme the government, bosses, friends, enemies? Anything, just to blame the responsibility for your life on the "circumstances".

Correcting mistakes, we find peace in the soul, create and grow spiritually. And if instead we choose indulging, "exhaust" - zero, problems are not solved, conscience is tormented, and such "happiness" can last as long as you like.

The notorious self-esteem

In almost any particular case, the real problem is not an event, but our hesitating self-esteem. Almost everything that we say and do in an informal setting can be reduced to the assertion of our own importance. Every word is an absurd show of dust against the backdrop of eternity. And this text is no exception.

In any situation, we are able to come up with thousands of excuses in order to maintain the appearance of our importance. We act to prove our importance. We are inactive and remain passive, so that change does not disturb our overvalued conceit.

We indulge when our authority is in jeopardy, and we are twisted out in all inconceivable ways to justify and maintain this authority. We are doing everything to protect our far-fetched serious ideas about our own majestic person. Any situation where simple decisions and actions are replaced by emotional reasoning is a clear sign of indulgence, which justifies the feeling of one's unreasonable importance.

If you can't take yourself by the scruff of your neck and pull the circumstances out of the swamp, there is one more option for a psychologically healthy person to continue to exist. If problems are not solved, it is not necessary to worry about it. We cannot be in time everywhere and in everything, but more often than not we simply do not want this. If the problem is not solved, what is the point of indulging in idle? It is advisable to reconcile and calm down. You can do something - do it. You can't - live on and don't worry about anything.

Passively justify, reconcile and calm down, or actively act - the choice is yours.

Responsibility and irresponsibility for one's life

Sometimes one has to act forcefully, not of one's own free will, but because it is "necessary", because you are a poor, unfortunate victim of circumstances who have no choice, and therefore there is no responsibility either for yourself or for your own a life. At such moments, you live under duress, under the blows of a whip, which are inflicted by the wagon of fate.

You make such a choice yourself in order to blame the government, the authorities, parents, friends, the casual oncoming person - anyone, just to close your eyes to your own contribution to your life. So you hide from the "bitter" truth about yourself as a weak infantile person, avoid difficulties, do not solve the problem, and make yourself a victim of circumstances, which we must justly regret and reward for the damage suffered.

The position of the victim is a state when you assure yourself that there is no choice, but there are obligations that bind hand and foot. Having become a victim, you act not by choice, but when you must and must - that is, from hopelessness.

The victim does not choose to act. She "needs" to act, because life is pressed and circumstances force.

Everyone wants something from this person, they are waiting for something, everyone is tired of him for a long time, while he himself does not want to decide anything, but only wants to relax and have fun. And considers any obstacles to the desired, as one big compulsion to crawl out of the comfort zone.

And so the majority lives. People push themselves into office plantations in the morning, because they have "no choice", but only forced labor. All my life they pull the strap, not realizing that this was their own choice, dictated by internal contradictions.

All this slavish compulsion ends exactly at the very moment when you realize that you yourself have chosen to live like this. And if you haven't accepted responsibility for the choice, and you wait for life to improve, real growth opportunities go unnoticed.

And the position of the victim, and responsibility - just a mental feint - a way of thinking. The victim's position is chosen for the secondary benefit - to blame the events of his life on an external authority. Say, let the "guilty" repent, and already begin to improve our lives ...

Pay attention to what a childlike approach it is to scoff, or to burst into tears so that someone out there sees the injustice happening to us and starts to console us.

The victim does not know how to act. She expects that everything will work out, settle down and settle down somehow by itself, without her active participation. But nothing sensible usually spontaneously happens. Changes for the better require conscious effort. Miracles, inheritances and other gifts of fate are not taken into account. In general, life changes when you yourself move in the desired direction.

Making choices can be scary - these are real changes for which you are responsible. But this is the only way to grow up and get out of the state of the eternal victim, unable to control his life.

Independence and responsibility - this is not an easy way of growing up.

Swollen majesty

You are terribly attached to habitual, hackneyed paths, because you feel like an advanced "user" on them - the king of insignificant cubic centimeters of "comfort".

Avoid responsibility for your life when you don't want to realize who you are and what you deserve. Avoid responsibility, and blame others to maintain a bloated self-esteem that the truth would smash into chips.

Yes, once again it comes down to self-esteem. Everyone loves to overstate her. Don't feed bread, give only an excuse to feel cool and in demand. And then, when imbued with the illusion of his greatness, it becomes scary to lose it. And in such moments you surrender, flee from reality, take off your responsibility for your mistakes and become a victim of circumstances.

So a bad dancer refuses to admit the facts, begins to philosophize and rationalize: shoes are squeezed, he hasn't slept, the floor is slippery, envious people have interfered, he's not lucky. Any excuses count. Just to believe in them yourself.

So you hide from the truth, you assure yourself that you are really smart and important, and others are to blame for all problems ... Trying to keep your high self-esteem intact, because it's easier to be offended by life than to acknowledge your contribution to the situation.

Any self-justification suitable for self-deception is enough for self-deception. So you create an internal schism in order to maintain the illusion of your own greatness, and stop in development.

But you know the truth behind the scenes, and you are terribly afraid of it ...

Secretly, you know your deception. And on the surface of consciousness you continue to lie to yourself and you will be ready to "strangle" anyone who hints at this self-deception. You will defend your lies with foam at the mouth.

In the comfort zone you get stuck when the changes jeopardize the unreasonably swollen greatness. Suppressed truth creates neurosis.

Healing requires recognition of the truth. Only you yourself are responsible for yourself and your life.

Forcedness

Forcedness, hopelessness and commitment are one big illusion. All this is your real choice, dictated by doubts and internal contradictions. You always choose to live the way you live.

If homework is forced to tidy up without offering other options, there is still a choice. You can consciously abandon cases and accept the consequences. You can consciously agree to do the cleaning. In any case, you make a choice. And if you're not used to being responsible, even in such an innocent situation you will become a victim of circumstances.

So even a small service can turn out to be a grave suffering because it is perceived as a forced burden - a problem that they did not hesitate to blame on a weak-willed serf. And now, having no choice, it is necessary, resisting life, to do his slave labor, to pull someone else's burden. And then - quietly resent someone else's "arrogance", dreaming of raising a rebellion against the whole world.

One sober look at the situation is enough to see all its absurdity. When you are asked to do something, this is the moment you make a choice. And this choice is always there. You can refuse, you can pretend to be a fool, run away, snarl, you can fulfill the request. It's enough to admit what choice you want to make. Not forced, but want! An honest, balanced "I want" in any situation frees me from far-fetched coercion.

"Must" and "I want"

Yes, there are limitations in life. You are a man, not a deity. You can't create any coveted conditions. You can go to the point of absurdity and begin to resent the compulsion to breathe air, eat food and relieve yourself. These are the given of life - it remains to accept them calmly.

And problems arise where inevitable realities are confused with ordinary everyday difficulties. So their reluctance to do anything is taken for an impossible impossibility.

A sober "can not" indicates a real limitation. But sometimes it's "I can't" neurotic, when you justify the unwillingness to do business by an external supposedly "restriction". Say, and the mountains would have turned, if they had woken up during the time ... That is the position of the victim of circumstances.

You cannot become a deity - it is true. And it makes no sense to worry here. And if you worry that you can't quit smoking, it's already a neurosis by which you justify your unwillingness to quit smoking.

The statement that you cannot quit smoking implies that you can not quit. You just don't want to admit your real desire to smoke.

Any "want" can turn into "necessary" when the case is more complicated than expected. If you give up and don't want to continue, it is precisely this reluctance that we should take for granted, and not torment ourselves for our weaknesses. If the matter turned out to be more complicated, it's better to immediately admit your "I don't want" rather than deceive me with a lying "I can't".

Emotional "necessary", "I can't" and "forced" are neuroses, in situations where you refuse to take responsibility for your choice, appealing to your supposedly limitations.

Can't go in for sports? Do not make yourself a victim. Just calmly admit that you can score a sport.

Responsibility is an honest recognition of the consequences of one's own decisions, self-awareness as the main cause of what is happening with oneself. Avoiding responsibility for one's life means being stuck in emotional childhood, endless resentment and torment.

Being responsible means simply noticing that you always do what you want and get the natural consequences of your choice.

Self-deception

The root of the problem is our negative emotions. In this sense, all that really bothers us is not events, but excessive objectionable experiences. Initially, there is no objective need to worry about events. You can do something, get ready, fix it - great. You can't move on.

That is, in general, it is always enough to simply act. And there is no need to suffer psychologically at the same time. Even the disadvantaged and the injured do not need our experiences, but concrete practical help. All the same, there is no way to help whining the matter - only you yourself suffer and spoil the mood of others.

To understand, even at a logical level, this futility of negative experiences is the first step on the path to calm. Just a little step, because this does not end there. When mental pain ceases to be justified and appropriate, its intensity really slows down. But ...

Somewhere here we all stumble. If everything was so simple, then there would be no ground for prolonged conflicts, scandals, all kinds of mental torment and maya. It seems like he realized that it makes no sense to worry - and you live on in harmony.

And not just because the emotions are formed not from some obvious, balanced need, which you can calmly disbelieve, but irrationally, from the depths of the unconscious (here I refer again to the previous article).

Therefore, no matter how much a person wants to cope with their experiences, simply taking and deciding to calm down may not have any effect whatsoever. And to cut the roots of emotions with deceptive ease with the help of one understanding of their inappropriateness and futility, we can only hypothetically, talking about other people's feelings.

Clients, describing their problems, often say that it's logical that everything is clear - and you don't have to worry, but deep down something gnaws, torment continues. And in such cases, I ask you not to pay attention to your all "understanding" mind, put aside all its explanations aside, and start expressing the very same thing, irrational, torn from the depths, no matter how ridiculous and childish it may sound. And this is a fundamentally important point in psychological analysis.

For example, when you understand that there seems to be nothing to blame yourself for, but nevertheless torment you, you should stop trying to persuade yourself and express your guilt exactly as it sounds - to express, at least mentally to yourself, what you are worried about .

Partiality and self-deception

It is not easy to listen to emotions and to reveal them - they are too vague and indistinct, seem independent, as if they do not conceal any hidden background. And they are expressed in their very essence quite primitively in the form of unconditional, impenetrable correctness, as infallible axioms that are supposed to be simply believed, with short slogans in the spirit: "Must!", "You can't!", "That's right!"

This happens because emotions embody hard-to-understand desires, the achievement of which, if you look closely, there can be no strategic benefit to life at all. But these desires are strong, charged, and doubting them is the same as stepping on your throat - I really want to simply fulfill them without any control, or even analysis.

And therefore, our partisan, "smart" mind is struggling to justify clumsy emotions by building up piles of false, sometimes frankly illogical justifications just because you want to! Even without really understanding what exactly and why he wants. Something is torn from the inside and makes you act spontaneously and chaotically, without any clear logic. We recall the analogy of a fuzzy elephant in a china shop.

That is, in order not to seem to himself so inadequate and uncontrollable, "without a king in his head", the mind begins to lie, and ascribe to emotions specific as it were logical and appropriate reasons. Like, "I'm not sticking out my importance here, but just talking like that" - a simplified version of widespread self-deception.

And if a person hints that the logic in his self-justification does not quite converge, he, as usual, begins to resist, building on the go all new additional layers of lies that cover the original truth, lost in the depths of the soul. After all, one does not want to investigate one's desires, as mentioned above, but wants to simply fulfill them. Otherwise - bummer frustration.

The protective mechanism of such self-deception in psychology is called "rationalization." The protective mechanism of (sometimes aggressive) resistance is truthfully called "resistance".

We never see our self-deception. We only vaguely guess about him. When we begin to see, it immediately dissipates.

We justify our emotions as blindly and illogically as we are able to not notice this own blindness. Therefore, the less awareness, the ridiculous self-justification, on which the mind is conducted. Surrounding from such inadequacy can be marvelous.

We do not want to notice our own bias - the fact that emotions with all their claims is not the truth of objective life, but rather our small, subjective lie, self-deception, obscuring reality with personal beliefs about how everything should be.

We glide along a fine line, where a small step that increases awareness, is about to reveal self-seduction. But to bare it, even for their own eyes do not want to. Therefore, it is easier to stay with a cloudy mind.

Sometimes, as practice shows, there is nothing particularly terrible and difficult to recognize in a real hidden motive for an individual for a long time. And this motive is hiding simply by an old habit. And the "problem" here is only to take a step towards meeting your resistance yourself, and finally, to see what exactly the mind hides behind it so desperately.

Honesty with oneself

How many problems all of us have when we lead ourselves by the nose - how important is peremptory honesty with ourselves. Such honesty ensures the stability of the personal picture of the world, and with it - mental well-being.

Indeed, in fact, most of the mental suffering happens from the fear of losing the usual supports of the mind. Self-deception in this perspective is an attempt to lean on something a priori unstable, prone to crash.

And if the realism of their own illusions of views is initially ultimate (that is, the worldview does not contradict reality, but coincides with it), then there is nothing to lose - no matter what reality, it will no longer disturb its own exact reflection in our psyche.

In this sense, spiritual harmony is the resonance of the external, "objective" and internal, "subjective" - a person and the world coincide, merge to the stage of unity.

Moreover, there is no need to know the whole world - this is impossible. Psychological problems do not arise at all from the fact that we do not know something about this life; on the contrary, they arise from excessive false knowledge.

Consciousness is akin to a pure mirror. But the mind, the master of dreams, constantly for us invents the familiar and understandable, the "dude" and the "right", filling the ideal reflection of life in the mirror of consciousness with its chimeras.

Emotions are pure dreams, sometimes having nothing in common with the real. All quiet and stormy emotional claims, grievances and whims - this is such a futile argument of a staggering ego with a monolith of reality.

Resonance with life is a natural property of our gut. In order to reflect reality, a mirror does not need to understand it somehow. The mirror reflects life spontaneously due to its original properties - and reflects calmly what it is, and does not try to fabricate some kind of artificial especially attractive reflection.

Conscious communication in conflict situations

Conscious communication is an eternally topical topic. This confirms my experience with clients. The theme is particularly acute in family relations at close range, where the rights and obligations by default are unclear to anyone, and you have to somehow differentiate them yourself. Therefore, as an illustration, we take the relations of partners with such a reservation that the following is relevant in any human interaction. We can say that the article is devoted to harmonious communication and taxiing out of conflict situations in a constructive way. Do not wait for easy solutions and a panacea. The degree of productivity of any communication directly depends on the level of personal emotional development. So, nothing comes of it from a swoop. But general recommendations and unwritten "rules" may sound quite affordable. We'll talk about them.

Tactful interlocutors feel how to communicate carefully so as not to intrude into the forbidden territories of someone else's spiritual space. Therefore, other friends do not quarrel for years, not because they are so advanced and conscious, but because there is nothing special to share - everyone knows and sensitively protects the mutual borders. To strangers on the street, our person is so, in general, to a light bulb - we do not expect anything from them and do not take seriously.

And the closer a person is, the stronger is his influence and the significance of each word. And this despite the fact that all mutual borders, rights and "duties" can be blurred and mobile. Therefore, cohabitants practice daily clarification of relationships, which boils down to trying to convey to a partner where he unfairly "counts" our person and where he allows himself too much. Therefore, the clarification of relations inevitably leads to mutual accusations and attempts to convey personal innocence by setting it to the rank of family law.

You can, for example, be confident in your personal right to receive a certain amount of attention and care. And as a result of the shortage - to feel offended by the offended, and begin to prove to her "second half" the presence of guilt on her part. The imposition of guilt is an attempt to make a person his debtor - that is, a banal manipulation for personal gain.

It is amazing with what persistent naivety we all sometimes expect a partner to admit his guilt, repent of wrong, and begin to become better for the sake of our person. But no one is in a hurry to feel wrong. I already spoke about the reasons for this "slow pace" in a previous article.

As a result, while the topic of communication is neutral, everything is in order. But as soon as something meaningful comes up, the partners immediately strain their ears and begin to "scan" each other to understand whether the time has come for combat readiness, or while you can relax and breathe out.

Defaults

It is important to understand that there are no default rules in a relationship. Social dogmas are too shaky, blurry, and contradictory. Therefore, no one knows how to "properly" practice relationships simply because there are no invariably true standards for imitation here.

Everyone acts by touch under the influence of a personal code. But not everyone understands that this code is just personal, and not some kind of real universal law. Therefore, the imposition of one's opinion on what and in what amounts are owed to us is nothing other than the forced planting of one's own subjective charter into the partner's brain.

So I hear the protest - they say, "it's clear that a person should and must do it anyway ..." The following is a list of those very subjective laws of an impenetrable personal code. Purely human, I can understand the various claims of an individual. But they do not cease to be subjective from this.

In fact, by establishing mutual rules, we all simply agree, take risks and believe. Such conditional contracts do not provide any stable duty that the partner is "obligated" to fulfill. And if our expectations are not fulfilled, then they were not realistic. So, somewhere our person was deceived, confusing hopes with a ruthless reality.

"Nothing personal, just business"

In a recent article on treason and fidelity, I have already said that relationships are much like collaboration between business partners. As long as cooperation is mutually beneficial, it lives and grows stronger. As soon as at least one of the parties ceases to understand why she needs this "cooperation", relations fall apart.

A business analogy may seem unsuccessful because marital relations are built on personal sympathy and antipathy. But in reality, sympathy is nothing but the beneficial side of "business," and antipathy is unprofitable. We do not love our partner unconditionally, but to our advantage for specific positive talents and qualities. At progressman.ru, a recent article on the "duty" of love is devoted to this topic.

So, try to imagine an intelligent businessman, for whom cooperation with a partner has ceased to be profitable. How will he react? Will he begin to whine and lament, invoking his partner to justice? Or maybe he will get drunk and seek solace from friends, or parents? Or maybe she will shut herself in and devote time to a depressive study of patterns on the ceiling?

See what I'm getting at? A sensible businessman is practical, and unprofitable cooperation either reorganizes, transforming into profitable, or ends as exhausted. And there is no place for children's grievances in a mature relationship. "Only business".

And if everything is more or less clear with the cessation of cooperation (it's a simple business), then the transformation of unprofitable relations into profitable ones is a whole science that everyone masters on his own skin. This "Science" ideally answers the most difficult questions about how to harmonize negative communication and learn how to taxi crisis situations into a peaceful direction.

Litigation

Probably one of the first signs when it is time to "catch oneself by the tail" so that peaceful communication does not go into hostilities - this is when there is a desire to prove something to the interlocutor. The motive may look the most innocent - they say "we just talk like that" when, in fact, it is led by the good old "instinct" of the ego - a thirst for rightness. As soon as you felt that you want to explain something to a person, or prove it - that's all, the exchange of information has ended and self-affirmation has begun.

If the partner does not agree, then our obsessive arguments and evidence are perceived by him as mental violence. Around this way, most of all conflict situations begin. We naively seek respect and love, and in return we get the opposite - a natural "counterattack". Forcibly sweet, really, you won't.

The main problem of the relationship is not even that the partners have a different understanding of mutual rights and obligations, but that the partners arrange litigation instead of peace negotiations. That is, instead of clarifying mutual feelings and somehow negotiating, they are accepted to blame, hastily hoping thus to punish the "culprit" with "a fine and correctional labor."

The partner of such agility is unpleasantly surprised and perceives it as personal oppression, or even an arrogant demonstration of dislike and disrespect, as if he was being held for disenfranchised burdock, obliged to thank for the fact that they "let me go" at all.

Resentment, anger, accusations - all this does not lead to a profitable partnership, but to its collapse on the basis of mutual hatred. In this we should personally be accountable so that there is complete clarity of what exactly our person achieves by resorting to child manipulation in the hope of easy "profit".

As soon as communication begins to be controlled by emotions, the whole construct is instantly eroded from it, and each word is dedicated only to justification and proof of its innocence. Therefore, communicating in elevated tones, partners stop listening to each other. What kind of understanding of the interlocutor can we talk about when everything inside burns from the desire to be heard and justified in their claims?

In emotional communication, the exchange of information is replaced by direct, crude attempts to achieve immediate satisfaction. The vocal cords can extract many smart, beautiful meanings, guided by a "primitive" motive - to achieve superiority over the interlocutor. In this situation, instead of many words, it would be much more honest to simply repeat: "I'm right! I'm right!"

Vainness

Sometimes it seems that people simply forget how painful it was for them to get involved in another conflict, and again they step on the old rake. They hope for a utopian triumph of personal justice, but get a natural bruise on their forehead.

When both partners are "on fire", one should be aware of what the pouring of "oil" of additional "evidence" of their own right leads to. If neither side recedes, emotions intensify, and the conflict grows like a tornado, drawing all the energy of the participants into itself. The stronger this destructive element, the more directly and openly personal superiority is instilled by belittling the importance of the opponent, up to and including assault.

Other "interlocutors" are satisfied with the option - to squeeze and finish off a partner so that he retreats, even out of fear. That is how they become the heroes of criminal chronicles. The bestial methods of achieving satisfaction saturate the "bestial" layers of the psyche, while the "human" part suffers from shame and frustration.

It is important to understand that in a conflict of communication a person expresses in words not some truth, but the energy of his emotions. "Nothing personal". Therefore, it makes no sense to take what has been said to your account, rush to conclusions and make serious decisions in the heat of passion. Decisiveness seasoned with intoxicated anger inevitably leads to destruction. When emotions subside, the situation changes dramatically.

You can trust until the very end that a conflict-based clarification of relations will lead to some right conclusions, and our "correct" understanding of the situation will nevertheless reach the partner. But in fact, the most valuable conclusion drawn from the conflict is its complete futility - and even loss-making.

If the desired goal is peace, but in fact - war breaks out, then self-deception continues. If there is no understanding of the futility of trying to stay right in the eyes of the opponent in the conflict, it means that until you press it, either the "rake" is not so old, or your forehead is not at all a pity.

Understanding is necessary for understanding. And this is by no means a quarrel, where partners refuse to understand each other, where each is aimed at affirming his innocence. Emotional clarification of a relationship cannot bring anything else. If it is impossible to draw constructive conclusions in a calm mood, then hoping for this "miracle" in a state of passion is the height of naivety.

About unwillingness to listen

In one of the old articles with the heading "How to become smarter" I already spoke about two fundamental pillars of productive communication. The first is the practice of empathic listening, aimed at understanding the interlocutor, the second is the crystallization of thought, aimed at the task of being understood. Ideally, consciously listening, understands the interlocutor, and consciously speaking, conveys his own thoughts in a refined and clear form.

Both qualities are equally important, but the fact is that no one wants to understand, everyone wants to be understood. Even in the comments on the aforementioned article, almost everyone spoke and asked questions in the first part of the text, which was devoted to the clear expression of thoughts. That is, most of us want to not only be smart, understanding our interlocutor, but to look like that, expressing our thoughts beautifully and effectively.

The ability to speak allows the person to feel their importance. And the role of the listener to the majority seems boring and giving away a shade of diminished servility. Therefore, the majority listens in half an ear, impatiently waiting for the line at the "microphone" to convey and approve their opinion. In disputes and strife, this pattern is expressed especially clearly. There, other people's opinions become a complete obstacle to self-assertion.

No matter how humiliating the role of the one who hears other people's speeches may seem, in reality the situation easily turns into one where our talkative person, selflessly revealing himself, becomes something of an object of study for an attentive listener. As I see it, the mind is not so much the ability to express itself as the ability to understand - even if in silence.

Of course, when emotions are boiling, it is very difficult to step over the usual automatisms. But if the situation is pressing, and you don't want to develop the conflict, there is only one way out - to stop imposing your opinion. Further development of the plot can proceed in different scenarios.

A destructive option is to try to leave the last word behind you and with your nose up, slam the door. At the same time, the conflict sags in the personal space of the participants, where it can be exhausted, or can go to the stage of the Cold War, and swell up to great volumes. Constructive options, as always, are more complicated and require some skill.

Consciousness in communication

When everything turns upside down in the soul and the supports sway like during an earthquake, the first important step is not to panic, find an island of sobriety in your soul and ask yourself: "What exactly is happening? What am I doing? What do I want to come to? And what do I achieve by my actions in fact? "

When two argue, everyone wants to be heard and understood. To resolve the situation, someone is destined to take the first step, and be an adult for the inner child of his partner. It's about starting to listen to a person nearby really carefully. Do not evaluate, do not make excuses, do not argue, but simply see what happens, what the partner is in, what he is worried about.

That is how awareness is raised in communication, and condemnation with axy assessments is replaced by a voluminous understanding of the situation as a whole. These are two diametrically different positions. The main question of the first: "How to prove your case?" The main question of the second: "How to harmonize the situation?"

From the position of self-affirmation, a person, in general, is not inclined to think about something, but being blinded by emotions, he becomes a hostage of his "rightness". The whole clumsy conviction leaves the position of understanding and the situation becomes "voluminous" with many nuances. It may open up where and in what experiences the partner is stuck, how unrealistically difficult it is for him to calm down, and look at what is happening with our eyes. Metaphorically speaking, this is a transformation from an elephant bursting into a dish-shop - into a sophisticated connoisseur who knows a lot about dishes.

For an ego craving self-affirmation, such a maneuver may seem impossible - especially in a conflict situation, where on the contrary, you painfully want to make a partner a silent mouthpiece for your own moralizing. This desire weakens as one realizes its futility.

Yes, in a sense, I propose here to learn how to provide a partner with such a "service", the provision of which our person expected from him. Isn't that strange? Perhaps there is no futility in asserting one's innocence? Maybe it's easier to throw a link to this article for your partner so that he learns to listen? Say, "let him grow up, because he is wrong! And our person is right - this is what we must listen to! " Such arguments are a continuation of the old song about the partner's guilt and our eternal impenetrable "rightness".

In a long-standing article about self-importance, I already said that in a strange way, getting to know the mechanisms of self-deception prompts most of us to convict anyone, not ourselves, of delusions. Meanwhile, the only way of spiritual growth is connected with the knowledge of not strangers, but precisely of our own errors. And incriminating others in the presence of feelings of self-importance, speaks only of the swelling of such a person.

In the same way, hoping for the sake of personal whims that an adult will become a partner in a pair is a very childish position. A partner may, and will, only our infantile person will quickly get bored with him.

Resources for mindfulness in communication are easier to find for one whose consciousness is less absorbed in emotions. And this is not weakness, but on the contrary, a challenge that trains mental strength. When you exit the preoccupation with emotions, you are identified with the intoxicated layers of personality, and you get the feeling as if you woke up from a bad dream and came to your senses. If, at the same time, the ongoing drama causes a smile, this is a good sign.

On one side

We all sometimes don't like something in a relationship, and sometimes it's frankly annoying. But people rarely openly talk about the causes of their condition. And sometimes they themselves do not understand what exactly they are dissatisfied with. Everything is forced into the unconscious, from where it continues to influence invisibly.

As a result, you communicate with a person, and he is kind of nervous, twitching movements, intense look, stale tone. The man himself does not understand what is happening to him, but his dissatisfaction seeks a way out, and then the nit-picking begins to innocent little things.

You can pretend for a long time and that nothing is happening. But in the end, by virtue of restraint, negative emotions overlap each other, and create a ball of gloomy attitude to life.

To prevent relations from spilling over into silent wars, one must be able to talk. Do not torture each other, do not fight, but openly discuss what is happening and negotiate.

A destructive way of expressing emotions is their chaotic splashing out in impulsive attacks. Emotions can be expressed constructively - clearly indicating personal boundaries and feelings that arise during their violation.

In order for the partner to notice that they are listening to him, and not just nodding for a look, you can express what you heard in your own words - without distorting, without mocking - so that the person feels that they are really hearing.

If there is no strength for conscious communication, it is more productive to peacefully disperse in the corners and wait for the emotions to subside and the mutual space will cease to serve as a ring for fights.

There is a hard-to-prove Vedic concept based on which a woman sets the emotional background in a relationship. And men in general are emotionally weaker, and endure communication in elevated tones, which are much harder than women think. From this position, a man is like an empty vessel that can fill the energy of female love. When the vessel is full, the grateful man himself begins to love in return, and receives tremendous motivation to protect and support his woman.

Otherwise, men perceive women's attacks as disrespect and the struggle for power. In fact, a woman is not fighting for power, but for the opportunity to feel that same male support. There is logic in this, and vicious circles coupled with positives are easily traced. The grateful person thanks in return. Offended in response offends. A direct analogy is an ordinary mirror.

There are exceptions to any rule. All the nuances in the format of the article can not be voiced. And quarrels can lead to deep analysis and productive conclusions. Nevertheless, it is worthwhile to understand that in a relationship partners are on the same side, to each other are not enemies and not competitors. Therefore, a common boat should not be rocked, but should be strengthened with joint efforts.

Boredom and fear

We, as a rule, lose sight of the fact that boredom is not an event, but rather a condition.

That is, usually boredom is taken for some objective truth about what is happening uninteresting reality. In fact, one cannot taste the event and call it objectively bland and boring. Each time we taste only our own impressions of events.

Boredom is described as an unpleasant, passive and apathetic state, as if life around is empty and meaningless. And this is not a bright and pure Zen emptiness, but rather a kind of gloomy presence of something heavy and tortured.

Two types of boredom can be distinguished. The first is short-term boredom associated with participation in a "boring" event. The second is chronic, associated with participation in a "boring" life. Both types of boredom are caused by a stopper of impressions, and are expressed by blunted dissatisfaction, but the roots of experiences differ.

Short-term boredom

Short-term boredom is encountered when one's own state is in a dense dependence on external events. And now, if a person with such an addiction cannot squeeze out vivid impressions from the current event, then it is accepted to hurry what is happening so that soon the turn of something more exciting comes up. Therefore, short-term boredom is often accompanied by impatient irritation.

From this perspective, boredom is a reluctance to be satisfied with what is, and an unconscious claim to something more - a kind of childish statement in the right to better entertainment.

That is, a person discards responsibility for his own mood, and manipulating boredom, requires that he be entertained more diligently. All this, of course, happens implicitly and even unintentionally, and in the depths of the soul according to a long-standing childhood habit. Therefore, the bored person himself can feel his claims as an obscure exclamation to some abstract forces responsible for the program of events.

Chronic boredom

With long-term boredom, everything is more complicated, its nature is more global. She is a kind of germ of depression. Deprives the meaning of life, desires, and with them - and the forces to move and achieve something.

Such boredom is caused by suppressed fears, with which individual flows of vital energy are blocked. It is such a blockage that deprives one of emotional fullness, leads to a state of dissatisfaction and mental hunger for impressions - that is, to boredom. The stop occurs inside, in one's own unconscious, and a person can confidently believe that the whole thing is a meaningless, boring life.

No matter how exciting the external event may be, in a depressed state everything will seem empty. On the contrary, when it's easy on the soul, even washing dishes does not cause any boredom - the event is accepted as is.

And so, in order to unfreeze oneself from boredom and feel the meaning and taste of life, one would have to pay close attention to one's own fears that stand in the way of the desired. But looking fears in the face can be so unpleasant that there is always the temptation to circle yourself around the finger, artificially devaluing desires. Saying it's not a matter of fear at all, but simply achieving something is initially pointless.

There is no difference, there is a sense in our desires, or it is not there. The main thing is that the process of overcoming fear (on the way to the desired) itself releases psychic energy, and life ceases to seem boring and fresh. And desires are just an additional positive motive for this emancipation. And here, instead of intellectualization on the topic of the futility of everything and everything, it's enough to take and at least try something really. It will not be boring.

If desires are blocked so deeply that they are not felt, it is enough to take a few careful steps to meet fear. Then more and more. It is not necessary to undertake something dangerous to health. The life of most of us is already full of relatively safe opportunities that we are irrationally afraid of. Fear of the scene, fear of mistakes, great responsibility, new acquaintances, new places, all kinds of personal phobias - whatever it is, any challenge carries the gift of expanding borders.

Growing up and boredom

As I see it, boredom is one of the mechanisms of growing up. When we grow out of children's entertainment, we naturally lose interest in them. And at the stages when the old "children's" games no longer deliver, and the new ones have not yet been opened, the very lack of impressions may be felt - boredom. This means that something inside is asking for more responsibility - new, more global challenges beyond the everyday rut.

In this sense, all that fascinates us is such games of the current stage of mental development, including, career, spirituality, relationships, life, parenting, etc.

As an option, to overcome boredom, it is not necessary to expand the comfort zone, but you can take a step back and regress to the previous stage - dumb to the stage of yesterday's interests. This business is facilitated by monotonous entertainment, where one does not have to think and be sensitive: simple computer games, TV shows, Internet surfing, drugs.

If you still do not want to degrade, the mind, like the body, must be kept in good shape, providing new challenges. Constant development requires a constant challenge - the very obstacle that requires readiness to face fear.

To participate in new, more mature games can be both exciting and scary, but to stay in place means to deceive yourself, reveling in a painful emptiness. It seems that Abraham Maslow said somewhere that unrealized potential is almost the main cause of human suffering.

Choice and spontaneity

At the level of the thinking person there is a choice. At the level of contemplative consciousness, there are only spontaneous phenomena that consciousness contemplates. At the atomic level, there are no phenomena at all, but only atoms. The assertion that there is no choice is just as valid as the assertion that there are no cities, civilizations and humanity in general, because all this is just a collection of particles.

Another thing is that it is not so easy to check the illusory nature of life, because we are not able to perceive at the atomic level. But to feel the illusory nature of the choice is real. To do this, it is enough to enter into deep meditation, when the clarity of consciousness rises to the point where you begin to see how thoughts come. Absolutely spontaneous. The person does not construct them, but only takes them at face value, like a conductor.

Since childhood, I tried to capture and retain in my memory the images of dreams, remember the phrases that I heard from the characters of dreams. It felt like I had a personal magical pantry from where I could draw information independent of the outside world. In a dream, we are faced with an unconscious, free from personal will. Many are familiar with a state where thoughts, like radio, are reproduced quite spontaneously. In deep meditation, this state can become all-embracing. You feel like a pure presence in which all phenomena occur - the body moves, the mind thinks things are being done or not being done - everything just happens.

However, it is no coincidence that in most psychological movements the topic of responsibility for one's choice is one of the key. Modern psychology is not adapted for pure consciousness, it works in the interests of an identifying personality, for whom choice is like air. And so, when a person is imbued with clever concepts about the illusory nature of choice, she deprives herself of this air. I speak figuratively. But in fact, the concept of the illusory nature of choice, most people in some roundabout way leads to a state of apathy.

Most people are unfamiliar with the real spontaneity of all phenomena. Even with a deep familiarization, this theory still remains an abstract "mystical" concept. But the depressive state of mental impasse is probably familiar to everyone firsthand. In this state, it seems that there is no choice - not at all because his nature is illusory, but because the person himself refuses to understand that he has a choice.

A person in depression is like a voter in an election who suddenly realizes that no matter how he votes, everything has been decided for him a long time ago - and not in his favor. It remains only to passively inspect this sad performance. And the state of such hopelessness is by no means a real comprehension of the illusory nature of choice. Such hopelessness is self-deception when a person imagines that it is tied hand and foot.

The choice in this vein is of tremendous importance. Choice is a way to show that there is really no connectedness. Everyone at any time is free to do whatever he wants with his life, while meeting the natural consequences. And this understanding is a very useful thing that makes life easier, accessible to everyone. But to cause such an understanding in a person in the illusion of hopelessness is a difficult task. And if one starts to add philosophical disputes about the spontaneity of all things here, the task becomes almost impossible.

Both responsibility and spontaneity - both of these concepts relate to choice, but do not mix them. They contradict each other for the simple reason that they affect completely different mental components.

There is no choice at the infantile level, when the choice is terrible for its consequences. The choice is at a mature level when it ceases to scare. There is no choice again - on a conditionally "advanced" level, when its illusory nature ceases to frighten. The child must learn to make choices and become independent if he wants to grow up. And if you are "lucky," an adult will someday mature into the deep wisdom of a clear consciousness, freed from the illusion of individual will.

And if a person still hasn't learned to make a choice, it's too early for him to get rid of his personality! First you need to go through the stage of personality maturity. And philosophical discussions about the illusory nature of choice in this vein are just an excuse for their own helplessness and non-independence.

In a very real sense in life, everything is always in its place, everything is as it should be, because otherwise no one and nothing can. Everything is exactly as it is. If something changes, then life got to this. Each change, each shift in reality - feeling, thought, gesture - happens exactly as it should and in no other way, because it is an inevitable continuation of the natural course of things.

A new understanding arises on prepared soil. A seed cannot become a tree until it takes root in the earth, and does not go a long way, eating water, air and sunlight. Man cannot strive for creation until the soul for this is ripe. Everything follows naturally its own trends. Even chaos is governed by its inexplicable order. So what are we doing here, trying to come to harmony? We simply continue to follow the natural course of things, with all our contradictions, choices, doubts, because we cannot do otherwise. What is happening is the whole truth.

How to make a choice and not regret anything?

What to choose? Save what is, or take a chance for the better? Keep your "normal" job, or quit for a chance at a dream job? Keep today's "normal" relationship, or end it for the chance of a big love? To maintain average health, or dare to undergo a dangerous operation for the sake of recovery? Stay in the comfort zone, or start from scratch?

All these questions are real. Clients contacted me more than once. When you are at a crossroads, the fateful options are balanced and it is terrible to make a mistake, the exhausting torments of choice begin. The more significant the choice, the more difficult it is to decide.

The problem here is not the complexity of calculating the best choice - logic will help with the calculations. The problem is the fear of regrets: you know how well you can destroy yourself with remorse and are afraid of them beforehand.

When I was fourteen, at the party I wanted to invite a girl I liked to dance, but something was in the way. It seemed that I was simply obliged to approach her, and if I did not dare, I would be very sorry. I was so stressed that my headache - I tried to force myself to act, but it did not work out. After a few minutes of these torments, I saw that I simply could not decide - and it immediately became clear that I would not regret anything. This incident taught me never to regret anything. What exactly do I understand?

It then revealed to me that you do not regret the choice when you know that you could not otherwise. There was essentially no choice - there was nothing to regret.

And we started dating that girl five years later.

You regret what you did while you believe that you could have done otherwise. But what could it mean? Yes, there was a physiological opportunity. And there was also a physiological opportunity to win the lottery, drop out of the window, and become president. But there was no psychological possibility.

We easily forgive ourselves of material barriers. For example, a rock on the way. But in this chain of obstacles and opportunities we miss the psyche. No matter how small the mental impulse that incites you to choose, it is as real as a rock for measured seconds. Every little thing affects the whole universe.

How to make the right choice?

My clients were professional poker players. These are people who lose and earn on instant decisions. Each turn in the game can result in a huge loss, or a big win. I found that an experienced poker player does not regret losing if he knows that he made the right moves.

What does it mean? How can decisions that led to a loss be called correct?

The fact is that the player does not know the winning decisions - he is not omniscient. The player sees his own alignment: cards in his hand and on the table, remembers those who have left the game - and based on these fragmentary data he makes a non-winning move - he makes the most optimal move, which is more likely to lead to a win. And the player calls such a calculated choice the right one.

That is, the player does not work directly with a win. It works with probabilities. And if he chooses the optimal probability, then he makes the right move. He knows that he is acting at the peak of his resources and is doing everything in his power. And if he loses, then this is the will of fate, God, chance - choose to your taste.

A similar principle, I heard somewhere, doctors practice. It is important for the doctor to know: he did everything for the patient that was in his power. If the patient did not survive, then it should not have been - this is his fate and the natural course of life.

When you know for sure: you did everything that depended on you, then you don't worry about the perfect choice.

Now attention! We make every choice at the peak of current opportunities. Each move is optimal in the current conditions.

What does it mean?

Which is better - to earn a million, or sleep?

It would seem that you understand that in one situation you give more and more, and in another - less, you don't turn on, you are lazy. You can, for example, move to success, earn a million dollars, and instead work hard, distract yourself with entertainment.

The fact is that efforts do not necessarily mean a better choice. We are much more practical than we think about ourselves. Making a choice, we operate with something very real - that is, right now under our nose. We cannot choose to move to a million dollars - this is too abstract. We do not choose invisible targets. At best, we can take the supposed step toward the estimated million - this will be a real, honest choice.

Beautiful ideas about the desired sometimes differ radically from the real desired.

Imagine that you have two directions to choose from - step to a million dollars, or step to the refrigerator. The first direction is charged with a weak belief in vague success; the second - with firm confidence: "it will be delicious!". Therefore, the psyche so easily sabotages great goals - they are too ephemeral.

That is, we always choose between the options from the present before our own eyes. Here and now there is no option for guaranteed production of a million dollars. There is real rest and real work guaranteeing nothing.

You can romanticize the work, ascribe to it an aura of selectness, success and wealth - and then the motive to work will add weight - and it may become stronger than the motive to relax.

Once again: we never choose a goal; we always choose real processes here and now under our noses.

One of my clients once said: if we chose only the best sensations, we would not be distracted from rest at work. It seems like this is the most pleasant thing: to play, have fun, celebrate …

In fact, rest does not guarantee pleasant feelings. When you understand that rest moves away from the goal, it can be poisoned with anxiety - and will not bring joy. Work in such a situation will seem a more comfortable option.

Foresight

The choice is influenced by external conditions, self-esteem, foresight, clarity of thinking, belief in success. All these factors are floating, unstable. Therefore, the same choice may seem the best for today and unacceptable for tomorrow.

Every second you make your best choice based on available data. You do not see the whole situation. You know your cards - these are your resources, strengths and weaknesses; you see the alignment on the table - these are your ideas about the external situation. And you only assume what will happen next - what move life will make. This is all your game information.

Today, your knowledge was enough to get to this second by this person, to open this article and read to this place. Then you will make your next most optimal move.

When you understand that you are doing everything in your power, you have nothing to worry about. You could never have been otherwise; you have always made your best choice. And he brought you to this life, in this country, in such conditions, in such a body.

Sometimes your receptors make a far-sighted choice - useful in the future. Sometimes, because of unconsciousness, a destructive choice seems tasty. Addiction is psychological shortsightedness.

At the Crossroads

And what is all the same? Whether or not to decide on a new life, a new job, a risky operation, marriage? Which is better - even a small but real titmouse in the hands, or an abstract crane in the sky?

You can be known for scrolling options. You can question all the experts, hear a lot of opinions, weigh everything a hundred times - and get even more confused ...

It's better to immediately clarify: sometimes there is simply no perfect solution — and it's completely normal to choose the least evil.

If the choice is balanced, then it doesn't matter what to choose - try to catch it at least logically. You may not agree: how does it matter if the choice is of great importance in terms of consequences? But you do not have a point of view on the consequences. Therefore, you doubt it.

Imagine that the choice consists of two closed boxes - red and blue. In one - our duty million dollars - we do not know which one. In another - a rotten apple. Which box to choose? What do you think?

The correct answer is any box. There is nothing to think about. There is no difference between the two unknowns. In fact, there is no choice either.

Let's say an apple is in the box you selected. Will you regret the choice?

Remember. This move was not wrong. You always act at the peak of your capabilities and make your best choice. With your current store of knowledge about the game, you are already as effective as possible. You choose the optimal probabilities. And if you lose, remember - you did everything that depended on you. The end result of the game is the will of fate.

You are moving in conditions of limited visibility to a dim light. Choose the best you could see. Therefore, there is nothing to regret. Regrets go away when you clearly realize that you could not do otherwise.

In addition, a local loss in the next small game can be a stepping stone to a global victory in the big game. Yesterday's luck may turn into failure, and failure - even greater victory.

Briefly main thoughts:

You always choose the best that you can see. Rely on limited knowledge and experience. You don't have others.

You do not choose goals. Goals are too abstract for choice.

You choose the real processes here and now under the nose on the principle of reducing discomfort. You choose labor only when it is more comfortable than rest.

If you are exhausted by weighing the options, then you have already done everything you could - and you can choose any option - there is no difference between the two unknowns.

Maybe win, maybe lose. But remember - you did everything that depended on you.

You do not regret the choice when you firmly realize that you could not otherwise.

Comfort zone

Comfort zone is the edge of living space where you feel relative psychological comfort. Most often, it is a territory of predictable, familiar phenomena that relax and lull consciousness.

That is, the comfort zone is not some "comfortable" place with a soft armchair and soft drinks, but a state of "soul". The comfort zone is a pleasant half-forget, convenient for repetitive mechanical actions according to familiar patterns of thinking and behavior.

The comfort zone seems cozy and safe, but in reality it poses a serious threat that quietly turns the comfort zone into a quagmire of stagnation and wilting.

The expansion of the comfort zone as a factor of development

The thing is that in the comfort zone, you are not developing. When everything is more or less satisfied, most people do not feel motivated to act, make efforts, work on themselves. And if there is no reason to get out of the comfort zone, consciousness falls asleep, and a person quietly regresses. With prolonged stagnation, when you do not leave your comfort zone for a long time, even a small step beyond it can cause powerful stress.

A comfort zone can be imagined as a territory within whose borders you feel "at home". And if this territory is a small social "aquarium", then it turns out that it is comfortable in limited conditions. Then in life in general, it will be difficult to navigate.

Leaving the comfort zone, you move towards the unknown. And if the unknown is anticipating positive, interest is connecting. Otherwise, the unknown will cause alarm.

Going beyond the comfort zone is a step into a new state where mental support has not yet been developed. Usually, such steps are taken carefully so as not to fall too far beyond the boundaries of familiar life. Abrupt changes cause mental disorientation and anxiety.

One of the most obvious examples of expanding your comfort zone is growing up. When the child leaves the womb of the mother and finds himself in an unknown, frightening reality, his comfort zone as such is still absent. Over time, as the repetitive sensations live, the consciousness begins to fix the "familiar" and the child calms down. Gaining its first psychological support, the child's consciousness creates an initial comfort zone within which he feels safe. Further growth and expansion of the comfort zone for the child occurs due to the development of independence and independence.

Mental adulthood is inevitably associated with the continuous expansion of the comfort zone. This rule is true, including for adults, who often after twenty to thirty years stop growing up and begin to age. Children expand their comfort zone rapidly, as experiencing a huge interest in what is happening life. In principle, psychological maturation can take place throughout life. If you keep the mind in good shape, it can be improved continuously.

Our comfort zone is also our current stage of personality development. Being attached to the comfortable aspects of the current stage, we simultaneously cling to all its problematic aspects. A comfort zone fixes a person at a certain stage in life with all the problems that are peculiar to this stage. And in order to get rid of these problems, it is necessary to go beyond the comfort zone. A task whose solution goes beyond the comfort zone becomes a problem. Problem solving automatically expands the boundaries of the comfort zone, and advances on the path of personality development.

The expansion of the comfort zone turns the recent "problems" into tasks, the resolution of which no longer causes mental discomfort. Thus, if, for example, we have ten problems of the current stage of development, solving one of them can turn the remaining problems into problems. Expanding the comfort zone, we are surprised to find that once complex things become simple and understandable.

The expansion of the comfort zone is a kind of expansion of the conscious part of the psyche on the territory of the unconscious. In other words, expanding the comfort zone, we expand our consciousness. Solving external problems, we at the same time "conquer" new "territories" from our unconscious. At this time, various fears, blocks and clamps are released that kept the mind within its usual boundaries. About this on progressman.ru there is a separate article "Warning about experiences in the course of personality development."

The narrowing of the comfort zone as a factor of degradation

If a person avoids growing up, and takes root in the comfort zone, his level of awareness falls, the person becomes infantile, and when approaching the borders of his narrow comfort zone, he experiences irritability and anxiety. Drug addicts are deeply rooted in a narrow comfort zone, staying under the "buzz". When the effect of the drug weakens, the familiar world seems prickly and scary, because it no longer fits in the narrow comfort zone of the addict.

When a person realizes the danger of getting stuck in the comfort zone, the comfort zone itself (like a mental system) begins to include the internal mechanisms of development and expansion of its own areas. Typical components of a comfort zone, such as the availability of money, food and leisure facilities, can sometimes be reduced to having a comfortable sofa and beer in the refrigerator. And for some, this minimum may become the feature beyond which there is nothing more to strive for. And if such a person can afford to stay in such a comfort zone for a long period of time, he will experience rapid degradation. Alcoholism and drug addiction are simply short-sighted ways to "simplify" life, moving along the path of least resistance. The tendency to narrow the comfort zone is the road to nowhere, it is a regression in which a person gets drunk, loses his job, family, home and becomes a homeless person.

Many "drug addicts from spirituality" run away from life into the limited comfort zone that the "teaching" that devalues life offers them. Unfortunately, the devaluation of the secular, with the subsequent departure into the sect, most often occurs when a person simply does not want to expand his own comfort zone, when it is easier for him to fall asleep in spiritual illusions, instead of making efforts, overcoming his fears, and being responsible for decisions, recognize and accept reality here and now. All these measures are the true spiritual path, the development of personality and self-knowledge. Of course, for example, workaholics have their own extremes when it is easier for a person to forget about work than to solve accumulated psychological problems. Moderation in everything gives balance.

Leaving the comfort zone, moderately expanding its limits, without leading to stress and neurosis, is useful in all respects. An active lifestyle, playing sports, self-development, hard work - all this is the same path of least resistance. The difference between a drug addict and a healthy, "successful" person is only in the awareness of the possible consequences of his lifestyle. In the comfort zone of a successful person there are paths leading beyond it. The sage's comfort zone includes the practice of expanding the comfort zone. The wise path of least resistance is the path to accepting life here and now. Thanks to this acceptance, everything that you feel becomes a comfort zone. When a person accepts the present, his home is where he is. It is "rest in motion, and motion in rest."

Sometimes we have the illusion that it is much more comfortable and safer to hide from the world, and live quietly, "without protruding." But this is an illusion. True security is the ability to expand your comfort zone, and at least at a relative level, manage your life. And if, as a pet, or as a fish, you live in a cozy aquarium, an external source can break this "aquarium", and you will find yourself where there is no trace of the usual comfort. When there is a "habit" to expand the comfort zone, without clinging to the usual supports, where there is nothing familiar, it will be transferred relatively easily.

For life to become comfortable, we must be prepared for this comfort. We must be able to work on ourselves, even when no stimulus for development comes from the outside world. In the comfort zone, we should learn to develop internal incentives for development that are not dependent on external conditions. The comfort zone is just another way to remind us of our illusions, which sometimes seem sweeter than reality. Sometimes it's easier for us to forget and fall asleep in a "cozy" cage of a familiar life, or even on the run in everyday ruts, where we rush around in a circle, like a squirrel in a wheel. The moment of "awakening" from such dreams can be painful. Therefore, it is actually easier to stay awakened without leaving the true comfort zone, while consciously going beyond the false. The true comfort zone is the continuous development of personality and self-knowledge.

The financial crisis - the psychological crisis

The crisis is such a turning point, when the current supports for moving through life are slippery and unreliable. Usually this happens when the most significant areas are affected at the event level: work, hobbies, relationships. At the psychological level, basic convictions about oneself and external reality are shaken, which leads to the loss of a sense of security and predictability of what is happening.

You may have heard that in the Chinese language the word "crisis" consists of two characters - "danger" and "opportunity." The crisis leads to a state of suspension and impasse in which yesterday's tools for the development and achievement of what is desired become insolvent. The danger of the crisis lies in the temptation to give up and despair, and the possibility involves a fundamentally new stage of development.

That is, a crisis is always the loss of support, the loss of solid soil under your feet, like a path that you walk to a village was concrete, known and durable, and suddenly it turns out that it is not just shaky, it turns out that this path does not exist at all. And the path leading from this moment to the future is one sheer uncertainty. And is there any future there, in general, is unknown.

If a little round, we all have hardened "lulling" ideas about ourselves and life. When these ideas turn out to be untenable, a discrepancy arises. Subjective self-confidence and its trajectory of movement in life begins to strongly contrast with objective realities. Losing the ground under our feet, we lose the soothing sensation of an understandable, "normal" life. Consciousness is unsettled by engagement in habitual dreams. What seemed real and solid collapses overnight. And a feeling of "unreality" of what is happening comes, as if life is some strange movie about someone else. The mind, as it were, refuses to believe that all this is really happening here and now, and not in some kind of television plot. Everything is perceived as if from the side.

The stronger the clinging to ideas about oneself and the world, the more terrible is the breakdown of a person when these ideas collapse. That is, the crisis shakes all the usual supports, "forcibly" tearing it away from everyday soothing dreams. And then a person either wakes up, opening his eyes to the unknown, or closes in the comfort zone densely "shrunken" by new realities, leaving his head in illusion.

Based on personal observations, I can say that increasing awareness in itself leads to a personal crisis. Once upon a time there was a man, everything was in order with him, but due to some practice or emotional upheaval, consciousness woke up to such a degree of clarity where previous rationalizations about life cease to work. A person may feel that he has lost his understanding of life, when only a comfortable illusion of this understanding was lost. Such a crisis accompanies any kind of mental growth.

That is, in a successful scenario, the crisis prompts the individual to move to new pillars, to integrate with what is happening on a more subtle level. Theoretically, in the limit, this process leads to spiritual enlightenment in those very cases when the mind completely loses its ability to defend itself from life "here and now", but it does not split, but remains integral. If you do not bend the bar in an attempt to become a Buddha, the relative ease of being is still available even to the average man. At progressman.ru, a separate article is devoted to this topic.

In the "unsuccessful" situation, the person refuses to give up obsolete positions and closes himself from reality. This is fraught with a variety of mental difficulties: infantilism, intellectual and mental dullness, estrangement from oneself and one's experiences. The taste of life, desires, meanings is lost.

In general, I come to the conclusion that depression is nothing but alienation from oneself caused by suppressed anxiety. The experience of anxiety is so difficult to tolerate that sometimes it is easier for the consciousness to close it, hiding it in the unconscious. With this suppression, a whole layer of personality structure is blocked with all its desires, joys, goals. Anxiety is not felt in its pure form, but as a long-term muffled pain.

Anxiety to the unknown itself leads to believe that something terrible is happening. She connects the corresponding projections with which the person explains to himself what is happening. In the minds of most, the crisis is experienced as a vague sensation of a dark element in which one can easily disappear and disappear. A person feels as if there is a war around, and there can be no talk of any joys.

That is, a mental crisis can become a vicious circle, where anxiety connects the corresponding negative beliefs that further aggravate a clouded state. A man gives up, loses strength, throws significant things, and makes new gloomy conclusions about himself and his life. Apathy, guilt, resentment, fatigue - companions of mental crisis. That is how problems can pile up like a snowball if constructive conclusions and decisions were not made at the very beginning of the crisis.

The main problem of the crisis is not what happens at the economic level of the whole country and not even on the personal front of events, but how what is happening breaks our ideas about life and, most importantly, about ourselves. The crisis can be seen as a lesson in maturity in the school of life. At least once in a crisis it is useful to plunge headlong to see all the tricks of the mind, forcing drama, and to understand how harmful it is to take these mirages at face value.

Sometimes customers ask: "How to live further?" Somehow we live. The body breathes, the organs work, the legs go, the hands do, the mind thinks. No need to try to control everything. It's impossible. No matter how specific the situation may be, its successful outcome almost one hundred percent depends on the ability not to give up. The crisis pushes out of the comfort zone, in this - its dangers and its capabilities.

Satisfaction with life and the power of mind

Many people find satisfaction in struggle and resistance, and not in peace, in the activity of the mind, and not in its silence, in passions, and not in peace. And to be at peace with yourself and be present "here and now", they need enough good psychotherapy. And it is completely incomprehensible to such people why half of the religions consider a pacified state to be almost the peak of personal development, and in order to enter it, "it is enough to just meditate or smoke a joint". In general, as one friend of mine said: "such satisfaction does not satisfy me." The fact is that we are far from always in serenity, because we are not really able to control it - even handy stupefying drugs work unpredictably. But the development of the mind and mental recovery inevitably leads to a stable calm of consciousness and satisfaction with life, as opposed to everyday fussy activity. An awakened person will not exchange his tranquility and developed mind for any worldly benefits, I will try to explain why.

The power of discernment

One of the main functions of the mind is discernment, the ability to make choices. Black from white, good from bad, one distinguishes the mind from one another. The distinguishing ability of the mind is the main factor in the development of personality. I will say more, based on classical teachings, it is the advanced stage of the distinguishing ability of the mind that makes a person not just satisfied, but enlightened. This is possible when the mind becomes so subtle that it gains the ability to distinguish pure consciousness from everything else. "The difference between sattva (the substance of the mind) and Purusha (observer)" is one of the yoga-sutras aphorisms, which implies the distinction between the subtlest "matter" and the eternal spectator observing life.

When you clearly distinguish an object from thinking about it, this is already a fairly high level of the power of the mind (distinction) that advanced practices possess. The average person is able to distinguish only his own thoughts - one from the other, and his objects are distinguished at the subconscious level. The master is able to distinguish the finest facets of reality, such as: perception, existence, shades of moods, the source and core of experiences, etc. The strength of his mind allows us to distinguish and perceive the essence of things.

In essence, the development of personality and consciousness can be reduced to the ability to perceive more and more subtle causal levels of what is happening. He who sees the cause is able to deal with the consequences. And here we come to an important point. A person can find satisfaction in anger and envy when he does not distinguish between them, like suffering. That is, satisfaction from anger and envy is a sign that the distinction works at a relatively crude level.

What some people consider to be excellent conditions associated with struggle and resistance, for an advanced practitioner it may turn out to be a living hell if he is identified with this. Identification with the gross aspects of reality and the transition to more subtle ones is the essence of the development of personality and consciousness. It is all about refinement of perception and development of the ability to distinguish. Satisfying with gross, we more and more distinguish and choose the subtle.

At an advanced stage, the practitioner masters the art of self-liberation of any experiences, and then, in simple terms, he is able to afford any activity in any environment. Though you work as a janitor - if peace, freedom and bliss are in the soul, the nuances of external reality are not so important. Self-liberation occurs through insightful, relaxed, clear contemplation of the sphere of one's own consciousness. With this contemplation, thoughts and any mental fixations dissolve. But until this stage is reached, certain rules can be followed, for example: to avoid bad company, idle talk, sitting on the TV, alcohol and smoking, promiscuous sex, rough food. Personality development is a continuous movement towards ever more subtle levels of balance.

Visually, the power of discernment works in meditation, where the perception becomes so subtle that even rapture begins to appear gross, and then the consciousness switches to bliss. Then, when it is saturated with bliss, it is also freed from it, being in its true void form of absolute being beyond any sensations. Chitta-vritti-nirodha (mind-oscillating stop) is the goal of yoga. This stage borders on the transition to the subtlest impersonal level.

Cleansing

Suffering is cleansed, pushed to a new stage of life satisfaction. However, it is extremely important to wean yourself from the habit of indulging - to indulge yourself in bad experiences, otherwise there will be no end to suffering. When negative thoughts come, you should not pay special attention to them, then this information comes out just as a temporary experience, without affecting life.

Perception is refined by leaps and bounds, thanks to awareness and meditation. And such an intense refinement brings a lot of pain, because the mind, by habit, clings to the old attachments, while they no longer seem so pleasant. So, meeting old comrades, entering into conversation with them on once typical topics, one may feel discomfort from the fact that these topics at the new stage seem pointless and rude. Or, for example, outdated reactions may come up - such as anger and irritation, which at the moment are distinguishable as rude and dissonant. Sadness can occur when, out of habit, actions are performed that currently have no meaning. For example, a person turns on the TV, clicks channels, searches for something, but finds nothing.

As the power of discernment develops, perception buffers (blocks in the mind) begin to break through, and life is perceived more clearly and at times sharper. There is a time called the "period of pain", when it seems that life is simply impossible, and everything becomes one continuous suffering. And it is very desirable in such a period the presence of a person who has passed this stage, who could support. For some time, sometimes for a period of several years, the topic of stress release and neurosis opening may become the main thing for the practitioner.

Discrimination is an operation of the mind. Sometimes smart people are found, but their minds may lag behind. That is, you can be a genius of mathematics, a champion in chess, savvy in various matters, but at the same time not have the ordinary everyday foresight that comes through the development of the discriminating ability of the mind.

Returning to the question of why the awakened one does not exchange his level of development of personality and consciousness for any earthly benefits, I will quote Sri Aurobindo:

"If people could get at least a fleeting glimpse of that endless enjoyment, those perfect forces, those luminous spheres of elemental knowledge , of the deepest rest of our being that awaits us in the vast expanses that have not yet been reached by our animal evolution, they would abandon everything and not calm down until they possessed these treasures. But the path is narrow, the doors hardly give in, and fear, distrust and skepticism are always on the lookout - faithful guardians of Nature, preventing us from leaving its usual pastures. "

Personal development and self-knowledge are the true meaning of life. But real satisfaction with life is possible only when we stop chasing after external pleasures and find the source of peace and quiet within ourselves.

The development of intuition

I will try to explain how to develop intuition in this article using simple and logically clear examples. On a worldly level, intuition can be quite adequately reduced to sensitivity, insight, empathy and physiognomy. We simply begin to perceive life contemplatively, penetrating deeper into the essence of all phenomena. In a broad sense, the development of intuition occurs intuitively, that is, not by the mind, but with a direct perception of the occurring phenomenon at a given moment in time.

Imagine: you are sitting alone, on a quiet beach, and looking at the river. What will you see? Most people will not see anything interesting. What is there to look at? A river - it is a river. The mind marked the river with the river and rode on, in search of new experiences. It's boring to look at the river for more than ten seconds, because "nothing happens." The mind needs impressions: brighter, more interesting. Boredom is the main "block" for the development of intuition.

Now imagine on the banks of the same river some average bodhisattva who contemplates this river with her bodhichitta. What will a contemplative person see when looking at the river? He will see the same river! But he will not immediately put the label "river" on her. He will not dwell on this shortcut, and then skip to other "objects" in search of new experiences. The contemplator continues to look and see. He sees not just a river. He sees a fresh, always different "interweaving" of countless streams in the movement of the lapping of river waves and water bubbles. He sees countless worlds that are born and immediately dissolve in this spontaneous movement. He hears the "music" of the murmur, in which not a single "chord" is repeated. And the longer the contemplator sees the river, the deeper it penetrates into its world, up to the complete merger and dissolution of attention in this world.

The development of intuition is a look into the "depth" of what is happening here and now. The layman is bored when "nothing happens." Boredom dulls perception, makes us rush for more rude and "motley" impressions. Where for the layman "nothing happens", the contemplative gaze reveals the whole world! Not for nothing that "intuitio" in translation from Latin means contemplation. The development of intuition is due to the refinement of perception. Contemplation of the river is a good practice for the development of intuition. Any object can be suitable for contemplation, peering into which you comprehend its essence.

People have forgotten how to contemplate. We are waiting for us to be surprised with something interesting, or funny, so that our attention wakes up automatically. The consciousness of modern man has become lazy, coarsened and "snickering." The mind of the layman is clouded by vivid pictures from the "screens". On a silver platter, we are presented with the most saturated refined images lying on a rough surface. All that remains for us is lazy to swallow all this information chaos. Most people like pepper, sharper, louder, brighter, "more glamorous" to squeeze out the remnants of consciousness. Modern man has forgotten how to enjoy the natural taste of life here and now. On this topic on progressman.ru there are already a number of articles under the tag "sensitivity".

A similar process occurs while listening to music. You probably already guess why the youth can not listen to the classics? Classical music seems to most people "colorless", too boring. "Rough" modern music ("pop", "metal", "electronic", etc.) gives at least some (albeit rude) impressions. The same goes for food. Spicy sauces, seasonings, artificial sweeteners, dyes, concentrates, flavors: all this replaced us with the taste of "live" food. Also in leisure. At one extreme: clubs, parties, noise, alcohol, tobacco, many superficial relationships with people, a range of rich experiences. All this drains from us consciousness and devastates. At the other extreme, nature, a healthy lifestyle, clean, light, fresh and healthy food, sophisticated creativity, books, deep relationships with a narrow circle of loved ones, acceptance, understanding. These are the best conditions for the natural development of intuition.

All gross manifestations in all areas cloud the mind and dull the perception, which, of course, impedes the development of intuition. Simply put, the development of intuition is blocked when we "consume" gross manifestations of reality. Intuition develops when we try to perceive the harmony of more and more subtle spheres, in the interaction with which our perception becomes thinner. The development of intuition occurs most intensively when we intentionally practice awareness, concentration and contemplation. Refined contemplative consciousness perceives familiar images from "screens" as too bright, crude and saturated, and chooses sophistication. Only aroused attention and contemplation give the impression of the highest "quality". The more contemplation, the more a person gets impressions in any conditions, without feeling boredom.

When you feel bored, try to peer into this experience. Do not take it at face value. What is this experience? Where is it located? Where does it start? Does he have a form? Penetration into experience gives awareness of its subtle aspects that were not accessible to surface consciousness. Contemplative consciousness exposes boredom, "dismembers" it into more subtle impulses, the contemplation of which can be an exciting game. This is a valuable experience of self-knowledge.

The development of intuition is not a freebie. If you have serious intentions, a noticeable result may require years of practice. Perception develops so gradually that most often the changes are generally imperceptible. However, if you recall how you were half a year - a year ago, the changes will be obvious. It's like growing a child. The parent does not see how his child grows, because he sees him every day. And rare guests are surprised how other people's children grow up quickly.

Life is continuously flowing and changing. Intuitive perception is distinguished by sophistication. Contemplative consciousness does not see fictitious, and not "beyond." The contemplative consciousness sees what is. It just sees more clearly and clearly, because not chasing surface impressions. The philosopher Heraclitus said that "you cannot enter the same river twice." Mystic Osho argued that "you cannot enter the same river once." The river is changing continuously. She does not remain the same for an instant. The label "river" is a trick of a coarse mind that runs from boredom in search of new experiences. Awareness and contemplation lead to the natural development of intuition, because allow us to see the most sophisticated manifestations of what is happening. This is simple mindfulness when we, like a newborn, openly perceive reality here and now.